WOMEN, IDENTITY AND RELIGION IN WALES

Gender Studies in Wales
Astudiaethau Rhywedd yng Nghymru

The aim of this series is to fill a current gap in knowledge. As a number of historians, sociologists and literary critics have for some time been pointing out, there is a dearth of published research on the characteristics and effects of gender difference in Wales, both as it affected lives in the past and as it continues to shape present-day experience. Socially constructed concepts of masculine and feminine difference influence every aspect of individuals' lives; experiences in employment, in education, in culture and politics, as well as in personal relationships, are all shaped by them. Ethnic identities are also gendered; a country's history affects its concepts of gender difference so that what is seen as appropriately 'masculine' or 'feminine' varies within different cultures. What is needed in the Welsh context is more detailed research on the ways in which gender difference has operated and continues to operate within Welsh societies. Accordingly, this interdisciplinary and bilingual series of volumes on Gender Studies in Wales, authored by academics who are leaders in their particular fields of study, is designed to explore the diverse aspects of male and female identities in Wales, past and present. The series is bilingual, in the sense that some of its intended volumes will be in Welsh and some in English.

WOMEN, IDENTITY AND RELIGION IN WALES

Theology, Poetry, Story

Manon Ceridwen James

CARDIFF
UNIVERSITY OF WALES PRESS
2018

www.uwp.co.uk

British Library Cataloguing-in-Publication Data
A catalogue record for this book is available from the British Library.

ISBN   978-1-7868-3193-4
e-ISBN   978-1-7868-3194-1

The University of Wales Press acknowledges the financial support of the Isla Johnston Trust.

Typeset by Mark Heslington Ltd, Scarborough, North Yorkshire
Printed by CPI Antony Rowe, Chippenham, Wiltshire

I Dylan, Miriam, Catrin a Harri,
Mam a Dad,
gyda chariad a diolch

Contents

Acknowledgements

My grateful thanks go to the women in this study who shared so willingly and generously their life stories with me. Their resilience and strength has inspired me, as will become clear throughout the book.

I have had the privilege of being taught by many excellent teachers and lecturers as well as having been inspired by several people who have either made an impact on me from a distance or encouraged me personally along the way. I would particularly like to mention Christine Evans, Hefin Elias, Alan Hill, Deirdre Beddoe, John Sweet, Ian Stubbs, Jeremy Begbie and John Parr. This part of my journey was inspired by Stephen Pattison's book *Shame* which introduced me to a new way of doing theology that is both relevant and transformative. I was very fortunate to have him as the supervisor for my thesis and I am very grateful to him for all his support and insight which have made a huge contribution to this book. His writings within Practical Theology have been very influential to both my thinking and practice. I am also grateful to Chris Shannahan and Martin Stringer who contributed to my supervision and very much to my thinking and learning. Mark Pryce has also been a great encouragement to me in seeing the connections between theology and poetry.

Sarah Kennedy, Kim Moore and Nigel Jenkins were key influences as I started to find my poetic voice again and I thank them, along with John Fraser Williams, Gillian Clarke and Fiona Sampson for help with the drafting of some of the poems in this book.

I have gained much encouragement and stimulation from belonging to a symposium of feminist qualitative theological researchers. Thanks to Nicola Slee, Anne Phillips and Fran Porter in particular for including my work in their edited collections of papers arising from this symposium and for the help of many good friends made there. As well as Nicola, Anne and Fran, the following women have all contributed to my thinking as a theologian and researcher: Jennie Hurd, Allison Fenton, Alison Woolley, Kim Wasey, Ruth Perrin and Emma Rothwell.

I want to thank those who commented on parts of my original PhD thesis: Paula Yates, Graeme Smith, Fflur Dafydd, Dylan James, Dilys Williams and Ruth Russell-Jones. I was very grateful to them for their observations which helped me improve my writing. Ruth especially did a great job of finding my inconsistencies. Thanks especially to Dawn Llewellyn for her comments and help with the final draft of the book.

I also acknowledge with gratitude the financial support of the Isla Johnston Trust and Gladstone's Library. Much of the initial groundwork was completed during stints at Gladstone's and I was delighted to have received a scholarship from them which enabled me to spend a week there, and I also benefited from other brief stays at a reduced rate.

I would like to thank Menna Elfyn for her generosity in allowing me to use her brilliantly empowering poem *Will the Ladies Please Stay Behind* in full and for her permission to use her material in this book as well as her encouragement. I am also extremely grateful to Christine Kinsey for allowing me to use her thought-provoking and striking picture *Ymddiddan 1 / Colloquy 1* for the cover of this book.

Finally, I want to thank my husband and family for their support always – Dylan, Miriam, Catrin, Harri and my parents, Dilys and Brian. The book is dedicated to them as well as to the women whose courageous and inspiring voices are heard throughout the book.

Some more formal acknowledgments are also due, for parts of my work that have appeared in other publications. I gratefully acknowledge permission for use of the following material:

Manon Ceridwen James, 'Fat Chicks, Blue Books and Green Valleys: Identity, Religion and Women in Wales', in Nicola Slee, Fran Porter and Anne Phillips (eds), *The Faith Lives of Women and Girls*, Chapter 8, pp. 103–9 (London: Routledge, 2013).

Manon Ceridwen James, 'Song of a Voiceless Person: Using the Poetry of Menna Elfyn in a Study of Welsh Women's Identity and Religion', in Nicola Slee, Fran Porter and Anne Phillips (eds), *Researching Female Faith*, Chapter 11 (London: Routledge, 2018).

Acknowledgements are due to the editors of *Envoi* and *Obsessed with Pipework* where some of my poems first appeared. I am particularly grateful to Jan Fortune of Cinnamon Press (who publish *Envoi*) for publishing my first ever poem in a poetry magazine.

Introduction

All research is to an extent, autobiography. (Swinton and Mowat, 2006: 60)

What is the extent and nature of the impact of religion on the identities of Welsh women? This book is the story of how I attempted to answer this question. I explore the experiences and voices of a range of women and their insights into their personal and national identities within the context of a Wales which has, until recently, thought of itself as a religious nation. These voices come in a variety of forms: women I interviewed about their life stories and perspectives, the writings of several significant female poets and authors as well as the work of theologians, sociologists, historians and other theorists who have written about women, identity, religion and Wales.

Issues of identity, Welshness and religion have always been important to me. I am a first-language Welsh speaker, brought up in Nefyn on the Llŷn Peninsula, having studied, lived and worked in many different parts of Wales. I have also worked as a parish priest and training officer for the Church in Wales for over twenty years. However, the reason I started on this journey was not simply personal; it was also to understand how religion and Welsh identity had shaped the experiences of other women I had met during the course of my work and personal life.

One Sunday, when I was a diocesan officer, I covered two services for a priest who was on holiday and conversations in each of these two rural churches made an impact on me. Before the first service, I chatted with the worship leader who had a postgraduate degree in theology. When I asked her whether she had considered ordination she said that she was not 'good enough', despite being articulate and popular in the parish, with a Masters in theology. At the second service I spoke to another worship leader who eventually offered herself for ordination, who described the difficulties of finding her 'voice' during training and of having too little confidence in her own ability even though she was clearly highly competent.

This led me to reflect on whether there was anything in particular about the Welsh context which led to low self-confidence, self-esteem and a feeling of lack of agency. I particularly wanted to find out whether the religious traditions, practices and institutions within Wales had affected Welsh women's experience negatively, in order to inform my own church and training work.

Although being female and Welsh were important aspects of my own identity, they were identifiers which others found inferior, strange and amusing. I trained for the ministry in Cambridge, and often came up against prejudice for being Welsh. We were treated politely but it was clear that we did not fit in: for example,

I was bemused by the constant questioning about which school I had attended, when almost everyone I knew went to their local school. (Really, the question was which public school was I from.)

Ironically Canon Enid Morgan of Aberystwyth, one of the first women to be ordained deacon in the Church in Wales, also describes this experience, of 'feeling inferior on two counts', of being both Welsh and female, during her time at Oxford (Morgan, 1994: 267). For me, the experience crystallised around the debates about the ordination of women which were at their strongest during this time as both the General Synod of the Church of England and the Governing Body of the Church in Wales debated this during my period of training. We had to listen to arguments as to why God would not want women to preach or lead churches because of premenstrual tension, or because women's main responsibility was to be wives and mothers, not church leaders. To be female was to have a stigmatised identity and this was underlined in my experience by the rejection of those of us who were women in ministry by the small group of clergy and parishioners who were against the ordination of women. After ordination to the diaconate, week by week from June 1994 until January 1997 I had to stand aside during the communion service at the point when only a male voice could say the words of consecration over the bread and wine. Even for such a short time (many other women clergy endured decades of this) the experience had an impact on me. Although women can now be ordained and become bishops in the Church in Wales, it is still regarded as acceptable for those against the ordination of women to reject their ministry on theological grounds.

Did my own feelings of a lack of confidence stem from being female and Welsh? Are they both stigmatised identities? This, in part, is the story of this exploration. However, part of the answer to this question came very early on in my research. Negative feelings about the self in the West are widespread and not necessarily linked to social identities. For example, the experience of 'impostorship' is common within education, where both students and teachers describe an alienation, of feeling they do not have a 'right' to be either educated or educators – an overwhelming emotion that cuts across racial, gender and class lines (Brookfield, 2006: 76–83). In my own discussions with friends and colleagues, I have found 'impostorship' to be a common experience; even outwardly successful white men have told me they have moments of self-doubt and of feeling they do not belong.

If these feelings were common, I still wanted to explore them within my own context – and I needed a framework to help me do this.

A framework – Practical Theology and critical conversation

My own academic background is in theology, and despite the perception that it is a dry theoretical subject, theology has always been 'practical' in that questions of how to live out faith morally, ethically and within relationships have always been a feature of Jewish and Christian life (Pattison and Lynch, 2005: 409).

Practical Theology can be defined as:

A place where religious belief, tradition and practice meets contemporary experiences, questions and actions and conducts a dialogue that is mutually enriching, intellectually critical and practically transforming. (Pattison and Woodward, 2000: 7)

As the definition suggests, Practical Theology is an interdisciplinary subject and is concerned with making connections between theology and experience in order to make a practical difference in people's lives. Experience, of course, is a contested word – whose experience are we talking about (Llewellyn, 2015: 22)? Very often those who are stigmatised or oppressed have had their experiences and contribution ignored or marginalised, whilst the voices of the powerful are heard clearly. People also have several different identities which intersect in different ways – being a white woman is different from being a black woman; poverty, background, sexuality, ability/disability all position us differently, bringing privileges as well as challenges.

The above definition reflects the sense that Practical Theology is a conversation, and the other dialogue partner can be any discipline which deepens our knowledge of what it means to be human. Practical Theology has several strands reflecting on politics, public life, the arts and all forms of cultural expression. Research within Practical Theology can involve many partners, from the behavioural and social sciences to historical and philosophical approaches. Central to the discipline is the belief that theology and experience in all their forms have something meaningful to contribute reciprocally, in order to enrich our understanding of what it means to be human.

However, Practical Theology is primarily a critical subject in that its main concern is to transform church and society (Pattison and Lynch, 2005: 410), to 'encourage more thoughtful, healthy and authentic forms of living' (Pattison and Lynch, 2005: 412). Practical theologians also acknowledge that one area of critique is Christian teaching, and particularly practice as seen in the life of the institutional churches (Graham, 2000: 104–17; Swinton and Mowat, 2006: 6).

Pattison develops his idea of Practical Theology as discussion in a methodology which he calls 'critical conversation' and explains:

The basic idea here is that the student should imagine herself as being involved in a three way conversation between (a) her own ideas, beliefs, feelings, perceptions and assumptions, (b) the beliefs, assumptions and perceptions provided by the Christian tradition … and (c) the contemporary situation which is being examined. (2000b: 139)

A discussion is a 'living thing which evolves and changes' (139), with all participants (as in a real conversation) finding out things about themselves that they did not know before, as well as the other participants' points of view, during the course of a conversation. Exchanges like these can be difficult and costly, and reveal connections as well as disconnections. Finally, it is important that the identity of each participant and their integrity remains intact, and is respected (140).

I realised that I could use this (albeit simple) framework when I read Pattison's book *Shame* which, using this critical conversation approach, explores difficult feelings about the self and particularly the emotion of shame. He explores his

3

own feelings of lack of self-worth by describing his own story and emotions, and relates them to writings in sociology, psychology and history as a form of 'conversation'. He then discusses his findings in relation to theology itself and Christian practice and tradition, and then uses his exploration to make suggestions as to how the Church might address these issues (Pattison, 2000a: 11).

I recognised that this would be a useful method to help me better understand the experiences of women in Wales and how religion had affected them and their sense of who they are, and what part it plays in forming their social identities. My next task was to find conversation partners.

Conversation partners: the structure of the book

My first set of conversation partners form the background to this research. In Chapter 1, I explore identity as how we think and feel about ourselves and as both social and personal. I discuss some postmodern approaches to identity as constructed in language and practice with a brief look at the work of Judith Butler and Julia Kristeva. I describe how identity is also present in stories we tell about ourselves and the social groups to which we belong, including nationhood. After examining narrative identity I then look at the work of Manuel Castells who argues that identities can be constructed by those in power, as well as by those who are trying to withstand powerful forces, which is particularly significant in the context of Wales. I end by looking at theological voices, the feminist critique of the traditional teaching about identity and the self which has been particularly problematic for women, and the work of Miroslav Volf who writes about the dangers of exclusive identities. Chapter 2 also looks at some theories of social or national identity, particularly Benedict Anderson's insight about nations as 'imagined communities' and also the work of Carol Trosset who attempts to define a set of Welsh characteristics. I also refer to the postcolonial debate as well as a brief exploration of cultural cringe.

In the third chapter I engage with the myth of the dominance of Nonconformity, especially in the light of current discussions about secularism in Wales and the UK, and conduct a brief historical survey of Christianity and identity in Wales. I argue that Christianity is important for Welsh and English identities but for very different reasons, and that secularism in Wales is qualitatively different from other parts of the UK. It is arguable which denominations have been the guardians of a characteristic Welsh identity; at different times the various denominations have played a part in constructing Welsh identities for their own ends.

In Chapter 4, I explore the sociological and, historical context of images and stereotypes of women and religion in Wales, and, using the work of Deirdre Beddoe, look at the key tropes of the Welsh Mam, Welsh Lady in costume, Pious Woman, Sexy Woman and Funny Woman. We hear a variety of women's voices in this section, from women who took part in the Merched y Wawr Oral History Project to the artist Christine Kinsey, whose work *Ymddiddan 1 / Colloquy 1* forms the cover for this book. A key voice is the medieval poet Gwerful Mechain whose poem 'Ode to the Vagina' challenged me to dig further into the question of how the stereotype of Welsh women became so repressed and respectable when a religious poem written by a woman praised her own genitals. This chapter explores the controversial *Reports of the Commissioners of Inquiry into the State of Education in Wales 1847* known as 'The Treachery of the Blue Books'.

In Chapter 5, I discuss the findings and look at the common themes which emerged in life-story conversation-interviews with thirteen women. I introduce the dramatic story of Elinor as a case study, who describes her struggle to find an authentic faith and identity in the midst of coming to terms with the shame of illegitimacy, and being brought up by a woman she had thought of as her mother but who was in fact her grandmother. Other women's voices are also heard in this chapter – Jinny and Jessie, both agnostic, Stefania, Helen and Hannah who are occasional attenders in church, Lucy and Harriet who are Anglicans, Marged, Sera and Bethan who are Nonconformists, and Yvette and Stacey who are nonde-nominational Christians. Stefania and Bethan had a Catholic upbringing, with Stefania identifying as dual heritage Italian and Welsh, and Yvette is an American born to a Welsh family and now living in Wales. Despite their different commit-ments and backgrounds, common themes emerge within their narratives of repression, respectability, agency, belonging and alienation, class, motherhood, values and nostalgia.

In Chapter 6 I reflect on whether these themes also emerge in close reading of the work of significant female writers – Menna Elfyn, Mererid Hopwood, Jan Morris, Charlotte Williams and Jasmine Donahaye. I have chosen Elfyn and Hopwood because of their prominence as female poets writing in Welsh, and the memoirs as they represent a grappling with identity from different perspectives including race, gender identity and religion.

In my final two chapters I explore the findings in relation to our context and make suggestions for theology and church practice in order to contribute posi-tively to the flourishing of women's (and men's) identities in postmodern Wales. I also discuss issues that need to be addressed generally within Welsh society, noting that current constructions can lead to alienation for working-class Welsh women, and those who are not 'Welsh' enough according to a particular middle-class elite identified by my research participants.

A brief note about the research

The heart of this book is the experience and life stories of the thirteen women I interviewed as part of a research project. Here I briefly outline some of the deci-sions I made regarding these conversations, methods which I also used in order to reflect on the memoirs and poetry of the women writers I studied.[1] Another important aspect of research is to be transparent about personal and philosophical commitments. As a Christian, I believe that every person is made in God's image, deserving love, respect, dignity and freedom. As a feminist, I am also committed to equal opportunity and value to be given to men and women. For me, both these stances are about working towards the flourishing of individuals and communities. Therefore research is not a purely academic activity but should be undertaken in order to hear a variety of voices, not just the perspectives of those who have power and influence, as well as to make a practical difference to people's lives. These commitments also led me to research methods which focussed on people's unique and shared stories, which I now explore.

The significance of stories

An important aspect of my research method was to value the importance of stories. As I explore in Chapter 1, narratives can help create both national and personal identities (Riessman, 1993: 5). Storytelling is particularly strong within Welsh culture: myths and legends have 'sustained the very existence of Wales' (Morgan, 1986: 20). Theology also has a strong narrative tradition, from Jesus' parables to accounts of the lives of the early Christian martyrs through to present-day reflections by theologians on encountering God in difficult circumstances, even stories that are difficult to tell (Graham, Walton and Ward, 2005: 47–77).

These were persuasive arguments for me as to why a narrative approach could be useful in looking at the identity of women in Wales within the discipline of Practical Theology, and the reason why I decided to interview a small sample of women about their life stories as well as look at Welsh women's memoirs and poetry. However, I realised early on in my reading that there seemed to be little agreement about what narrative was, let alone how to use story within research (Andrews, Squire and Tamboukou, 2008: 1; Bold, 2012: 1; Riessman, 2008: 3), though there is some consensus that a story is an interpretation and a way of making connections for an audience (Riessman, 2008: 3).

So what is distinctive about a narrative approach? The main feature is the significance given to stories within the research encounter – they are not dismissed as irrelevant diversions but, rather, recognised as important in conveying meaning (Mishler, 1986: 5, 69). This means that often narratives are kept intact for analysis, are not broken up into themes, and that they are analysed within their context for ordinary, everyday understandings (Mishler, 1986: 5; see also Elliott, 2005: 36).

A key feature of appreciating the narrative form is acknowledging that it involves interpretation from the start, by the narrator herself in choosing what to reveal and the connections between what she is describing (Salmon and Riessman, 2008: 81).

This led me to decide that I would conduct interviews with a few common questions, but with considerable freedom to ask follow-up questions as well as seek clarifications. Following Mishler (1986) and Slee (2004) I preferred to put into practice equality as well as empathy and friendship at the heart of this process, and it would therefore be more appropriate to call my practice research conversations rather than interviews.

Foregrounding women's voices

As I have already mentioned, Practical Theology adopts different partners for its theological reflection, including the social sciences. This research is 'qualitative' in that it focuses on what cannot be measured, for example, meanings, relationships and stories (Slee, 2004: 9–10). This approach maintains that knowledge can be gained from reflecting deeply on 'unique, non-replicable experiences' (Swinton and Mowat, 2006: 43). It can also involve interdisciplinary and creative methods in order to explore more deeply the participants' experiences. Therefore, examining women's writing in my project is entirely consistent with this approach (Denzin and Lincoln, 2011: 6; Creswell, 2013: 45). A researcher's personal story and contribution as well as personal commitment to the research question can be seen as a strength within this framework, meaning that they can engage with the research participants meaningfully and effectively (Reinharz, 1992: 259). The researcher's reflectiveness is an important part of gaining knowledge.

Although I wrote in my journal during the time of the research and kept an occasional blog, the most effective way I found to reflect on what I was learning was through writing poetry. When I write a poem what develops often surprises me – new connections or metaphors emerge which are often unexpected. My poems also reflect my particular point of view, emotions and thoughts at any particular time during the research and through reflecting on them I can see how my thinking has changed. The poems that emerged during the research process are included throughout the book.

Choosing the women

I am aware that the claims I make for my findings are limited to the women I have studied in conversations and in literature. However, their experiences make an important and in-depth contribution to understanding about women, identity and Wales. I decided early on to concentrate on my own age group (30–55 year olds, 'generation X') in order to gain a richer understanding of my own personal experience and context.[2] After I had completed the interviews I realised that some social identities were 'missing' and so the memoirs are all from women who have particularly interesting and complex identities – Jan Morris as a transgender woman, Charlotte Williams who is Welsh and Guyanese and Jasmine Donahaye who is Jewish.

I deliberately did not ask anyone directly whether they were interested in participating (in case they felt pressurised in any way because of a prior relationship) but made it known through personal conversations, social media and denominational mailings that I was looking for interviewees. I was anxious about whether people would want to be involved, but to my surprise many women were interested in the project and volunteered to be interviewed, because they regarded their own story as interesting, or wanted to 'help' me in some way. Although many women felt nervous and unsure of how useful their stories might be and how effective their storytelling was, they also seemed keen to be given the opportunity to share their story and, particularly, to reflect on it.

Some who were involved in the research were known to me as friends or acquaintances and in some cases this had been a factor in offering their story. As well as wanting to help, some of the participants also wanted to make sure that their own particular denomination's voice was heard. All of those who responded were either Christians or atheist/agnostic. They lived in many different parts of Wales, town and country, north and south. They held a variety of jobs and the group included an administrative assistant, teacher, taxi driver, full-time mother, writer, cleaner and two social workers. A few held (or had previously held) lay or ministerial posts within Christian institutions. All, apart from two, were mothers. Most of the women were married or living with partners; four were single or between relationships during the time of the research conversation.

The research conversations

My first question was always 'Tell me your life story, especially the part that religion has played, if any, within it'. The question could be critiqued for assuming that it is normative for religion to play a part in their lives. However, in all but one case, the question elicited a long response. I also asked questions for clarification and to gather more information, especially to understand the participants' own meaning or reflection on their life events. I also had three other questions that I asked at some stage during the second part of the interview:

- What does it mean to you to be a Welsh woman?
- Do you think religion contributes to the stereotypes of Welsh women and how we see ourselves?
- Who do you think are the Welsh female heroines or role models?

These questions were designed to understand the stories, characters and archetypes which my conversation partners believed were important for Welsh female identity and the resources with which they constructed Welsh female identity for themselves. This often produced more exploration of their understanding of identity and Welsh female identity and occasionally more narratives. The question about heroines and role models proved particularly interesting.

After transcribing the interviews (either directly, or through translating them into English) I analysed the themes using the perspective of discourse analysis (DA), which I also used to reflect on the poetry and memoirs. I looked out for assumptions, keywords and metaphors, as well as the shared meanings which emerged about identity (Fairclough, 2003; Gee, 2011). An important concept in DA for this project was 'figured world', a phrase which conveys a typical and ideal imagined 'socially and culturally constructed realm' (Gee, 2011: 70). A figured world is partly imagined, partly enacted, however it is something which individuals engage with and is part of their reality. In this research I reflected on what I was being invited to assume and what was actually assumed in words, phrases and stories as well as people, language, practices, organisations, settings and objects (Gee, 2011: 72).

I came to this research wondering why women felt silenced and I wrote this poem in response to the feelings that I was experiencing. Throughout the course of this study I found that even if Welsh women experience a form of silencing, they have found other, creative and alternative ways to make their voices heard.

SILENCES

The silence that is frustration.
I am voiceless because I can't say that.
You would be shocked, disturbed.

The silence from not belonging.
I don't want to say something stupid.
I am not good enough to be here.

The silence when words falter.
I am only learning to speak, but I have to be confident
and strong before you will listen.

The silence because no one has said this before.
I don't want to be the first......
but I'll join in with you if you say it.

The silence from having two languages,
and the word has fallen through the gap.

The silence because I have so much to say -
where do I begin?

The silence because you have stopped talking,
and I have stopped listening.

The silence because I am full.
At peace. I am satisfied.
No need to say anything,
you understand.

The silence that comes from not speaking –
because there's no other living being.
I can't hear anything but the sound of my breathing
and occasionally my singing. (Ceridwen 2009)

1

What Do We Mean by Identity?

Identity offers a way of thinking about the links between the personal and the social; of the meeting place of the psychological and the social, of the psyche and the society. (Woodward, 2002: vii)

What is identity?

Crucial to this study is the point of view that identity is constructed between people, and in this chapter I outline what a constructivist rather than essentialist view of identity means. I also explore ways of speaking about the relationship between social and personal identity and theories which help us understand social and personal identity as constructed in behaviours, language and in opposition to an 'other'.

In wanting to study thoughts and feelings about the self I was originally drawn to more psychological concepts. It seemed that 'self-esteem' might have been helpful in exploring positive or negative feelings about personal identity, and yet scales used to measure this, for example the Rosenberg scale (Rosenberg, 1965),[3] fail to convey the depth and complexity of how people feel and talk about themselves. Although psychological concepts such as self-confidence, self-esteem and agency have informed my thinking, this study is interested in identity-in-relation: interaction between how we feel about ourselves and the impact on this from feelings about the groupings to which we belong.

In academic writing, a constructivist view of identity is uncontroversial (Redman, 2000: 9), yet in everyday life we tend to see ourselves as having a continuous sense of self (see Archer, 2000) and assume that our social identities mean that we will hold particular characteristics – for example women as caring, French people as romantic. How an individual describes their identity and the extent to which they assign significance to their personal or social identifiers differs according to each person, as does the interplay between the two. Those aspects of our identities which could be considered marginalised are the identities we will more readily attribute to ourselves whilst discounting identities which are more normative (Reddie, 2009: 39–46). Reddie tells the story of an exercise in which he defined himself as black but 'forgot' to mention his identities as educated and heterosexual. We also define ourselves differently in different contexts, using the different categories of social groupings, personal characteristics, key relationships, roles and even interests and hobbies.

As well as personal and social identity, an important final category, ego identity, is a useful lens with which to analyse identity. It describes our inner world, unlike the outwardly identifiable social and personal characteristics observed by others. Ego identity is '*one's subjective feeling* about one's own situation and one's own continuity and uniqueness' (Goffman, 1990: 129, my emphasis). This is a useful way of understanding how we think and feel about ourselves and the social groupings to which we belong, and how they relate to one another.

Identity construction: a postmodern view

Identity is a way of speaking about what is important to us about ourselves. I now want to explore identity as 'constructed' rather than a given, and formed through performance, language and through recognising difference rather than similarity (Hall, 2000: 15–29). I find this concept of identity persuasive, that it is always in a state of flux and is created and recreated within social situations.

Judith Butler for example argues that (gender) identity is created through the repetition of embodied acts (Butler, 1999: 43) and against the backdrop of a power struggle between men and women, an attempt to impose heterosexuality as a norm and a polarity on which men and women are made to situate themselves (40). She argues against essentialism and rejects the idea that women hold a common identity. There is no essential core of femaleness or maleness, as if there is a 'doer behind the deed' (33).

Butler believes that the distinction between the sexes is a social construction (9). However, she is aware that this might lead to the disembodiment of gender, again, as if there is a doer behind or apart from the body, which she maintains is itself a social construction (12) and a 'set of boundaries, individual and social, politically signified and maintained' (44). Different contexts as well as other social identities intersect with that of gender and so it is impossible to separate women as a distinct category from all others (6).

Gender 'trouble', the name of Butler's book, stems from the resulting distress to those who cannot easily fit into these simplistic male–female heterosexual categories (xi). Gender is always an action and can never be set apart from the experience of actual people who find themselves, despite being a particular biological sex and sociological gender, held up against certain norms, values and expectations (33). Although these identifications can be helpful for identity politics, particularly in the fight for minority rights, they are ultimately destructive because power is then given to the majority to name (and therefore control and subjugate) the 'Other' (13).

Similarly, Julia Kristeva argues that the self is constructed within language (she would use the word discourse) and an understanding of difference. There is no self apart from the one who is already using language, constructing and in turn being constructed by it (Kristeva, 1984). The individual is part of a living and ever-changing context, forever in the state of becoming a 'subject in process'

(Kristeva, 1984: 22). The self therefore is in flux and constantly being created and recreated within social situations, within language.

I have found both writers' challenging of essentialism helpful and they have deepened my understanding about gender and sex. However, the questions that Archer (2000) poses still remain. If our identity is constructed and reconstructed through language and in (embodied) performance, how does this relate to our experience of being (or is it having?) a continuous self? The answer may lie in the concept of a narrative identity as a helpful way of bridging the gap between experience and theory.

A narrative identity?

Even within postmodern thinking about identity as constantly changing, the one aspect of ourselves which we can point to as being distinctive and knowable is our life story and the other stories we tell about ourselves (Elliott, 2005: 1). Our personal narrative is important for our self-understanding and interpretation of what it means to be ourselves (Taylor, 1989: 289). Stories convey both personal and social identity: as people construct and tell their stories we can understand the meanings they ascribe to events as well as their world views (Linde, 1993: 3). They can also help construct cultural identities in producing stereotypes and discourses that create boundaries and bond groups of people together (Loseke, 2007: 661; Riessman, 1993: 5).

Even if personal narrative then is a way of unifying the postmodern fragmented and socially constructed self, life stories themselves are also subjective. Freeman (1993) argues that in thinking about ourselves we are constantly interpreting and reinterpreting the social worlds and ourselves as actors within it. This also involves our (faulty) memory – we literally re-collect what we remember (6). Some of what we remember is 'fictional' as we are inevitably at a distance from the actual experience and cannot always remember rightly. As subjective beings we are aware that the distinction between fact and fiction in memory is fragile (11). We choose how and when to tell stories about ourselves, we choose what to say, and what to hide, some things we forget, other aspects we cannot help but remember.

However, there is still a dilemma. The self feels in our experience as if it is bounded, 'real' and something we can come to appreciate and understand apart from ourselves:

> ... even if my 'self', fleeting as it is, doesn't exist apart from my own narrative imagi-nation, indeed from my own belief in its very existence, it is nonetheless eminently real and – within limits – eminently knowable. (Freeman, 1993: 13)

Personal identity is experienced as 'real' even if we believe that it is constructed in language and performance and always evolving, because of our own life story.

In discussing whether what we 'remember' is fact or fiction or both within our personal biography, Freeman concludes that 'there is no historical truth outside of the narrative imagination' (226). He considers this unproblematic as he calls for individuals to have a poetic understanding of the self and its expression in constantly wanting to reinterpret and find meaning in experiences (222–32).

Narrative can therefore be a way of integrating identity within an acknowledgement of its constructed nature, and a poetic approach acknowledges the seemingly contradictory nature of both the mystery and 'knowability' of the self and the importance of meaning-making for individuals. Another important concept within postmodern theories of personal and social identity is that we notice and even construct our identity in difference, in opposition to an 'other'.

The Other

Kristeva argues that an important part of (personal) identity creation is what she terms 'abjection' – the expulsion of anything that is foreign, notably seen in the infant's earliest physical responses such as vomiting and defecating (Kristeva, 1982: 3) explained succinctly by McAfee as 'the state of abjecting or rejecting what is other to oneself – and thereby creating borders of an always tenuous "I"' (McAfee, 2004: 45). However, what is rejected is not foreign or other, but a part of oneself. This contradiction is an important aspect of Kristeva's theory:

> 'I' want none of that element, sign of their desire; 'I' do not want to listen, 'I' do not assimilate it, 'I' expel it. But since the food is not an 'other' for 'me,' who am only in their desire, I expel myself, I spit myself out, I abject myself within the same motion through which 'I' claim to establish myself. (Kristeva, 1982: 3)

This process is present throughout an individual's life-span and the desire to remain pure is regulated by religions (or even by art in non-religious societies) by 'conjuring up the abject things it seeks to dispel' (McAfee, 2004: 49). This is seen in the need to construct boundaries between different nationalities and cultures and defining foreignness and the 'other', though ironically this 'other' is intimately bound up with our experience of being ourselves, as 'the foreigner lives within us' and is 'the hidden face of our identity' (Kristeva, 1991: 1). The foreigner is us.

The dynamic of creating and rejecting an 'other' is not neutral; there are significant power and political implications when different value judgements are placed on different identities. An example of this is in relationships between nations, as argued by Said who comments that the West's relationship with the rest of the world is essentialist, simplistic and patronising, based on a 'web of racism, cultural stereotypes, political imperialism and dehumanising ideology' (Said, 2003: 27, 332) and Fanon who maintains that colonised people have been inculcated with a deeply felt 'inferiority complex' created by the destruction of their own indigenous cultures (Fanon, 2008: 9).

The power implications of 'otherness' are also gendered. According to de Beauvoir (1997) women are the ultimate other, and although she has been challenged for ignoring race and class her comment is still relevant, even if it is difficult to maintain the view that women are the 'ultimate' other given the relative privilege of white Western middle-class women:

> She is defined and differentiated with reference to man and not he with reference to her; she is the incidental, the inessential as opposed to the essential. He is the Subject, he is the Absolute – she is the Other. (de Beauvoir, 2000: 211)

Kristeva's theorising of the evolving nature of subjectivity within language has been important for my own understanding of identity, as has the construction of identity by creating borders, exaggerating differences and rejecting others on the basis of these differences. The political implications of 'othering' and the creation of identities are important to acknowledge. The construction of identities using religion and rejecting others and scapegoating them based on their social identities (including religion) is a horrifying and potentially violent feature of our globalised postmodern world. The backlash in the West against liberal tolerance, with religion used to create identity, justify racism and exclude and vilify people of different religions and races, is particularly alarming. It is vital that we understand how social identities are constructed and utilised, particularly by those with power and influence. The work of Manuel Castells is very helpful in enabling us to critique how social identities can be used and abused.

Project identities

Castells (2010) proposes three different forms of social identity construction which are also helpful. He suggests that identity is formed against the backdrop of globalisation, technology, the media, debates about the role of the nation-state and identity politics. He regards identity as 'people's source of meaning and experience' (6) for themselves, which they internalise and construct meanings within this internalisation using various cultural attributes and decisions made about their prioritisation (7). Identity can be distinguished from roles, which are more prescribed by institutions and organisations; their effect on a person is more contested, depending on how far the individual has internalised their role. The question of who constructs the identity and for what reason and with what resources and materials is key.

Castells states:

> I propose, as a hypothesis, that, in general terms, who constructs collective identity and for what, largely determines the symbolic content of this identity and its meaning for those identifying with it or placing themselves outside of it. (7)

He further comments that this always takes place in the context of power relationships and proposes three types of identity building:

1. *Legitimising Identity* – introduced by the dominant institutions of society to extend and rationalise their domination and constructed from materials derived from history for example religion, ethnicity, locality, nation.
2. *Resistance Identity* – built by those who are stigmatized or devalued by the dominant forces in society in order to resist and survive them. They are able to 'essentialise' characteristics such as geography, history or biology in order to bolster boundaries. It is a defensive identity.

3. *Project Identity* – social actors using whatever cultural means available not only to build an identity which withstands the dominant forces, but itself seeks to redefine their position and transform the overall social structure. (8)

Castells argues that in our postmodern world (or what he calls the network society) legitimising identities are waning and the effect of the nation-state on people's lives is lessening (420). However, resistance identities seem to have the potential to flourish and occasionally to allow for project identities to emerge.

Castells's work is important because it gives a framework and a language with which to understand and articulate social identity construction. Goffman's work helps us see that identity has three facets and that ego identity is a way of speaking about our thoughts and feelings about social and individual identity. Another relevant issue concerning social identity is that a strong identification with a social identity is not always beneficial for individual identity. Scheff, for example, argues for the importance to humans of 'social bonds' (1994: 1) and that bondlessness has lethal implications. He also argues that too strong a sense of social identity can likewise be harmful. Complete compliance with a group or nation's set of values and doctrines leads to the particular alienation from the self which he labels 'engulfment', because an individual denies important parts of themselves in order to conform totally to a group (2). Engulfment, like isolation, is a particular form of alienation and is therefore personally damaging (1997: 49). Identity is a complex subject, with political implications. How can social identities therefore be used for the common good?

A theology of embrace: Miroslav Volf

This dynamic of 'othering' that is present in identity construction has theological implications, explored particularly in the work of Miroslav Volf. Volf argues against essentialised identities because they have the potential for oppression and injustice, even war and violence, and he develops a theology of the postmodern, diffuse and developing self as consonant with a theology of human beings as made in the image of God.

Volf's work is also useful for a theological understanding of social and national identity in addressing the dangers of designating an 'other' in a potentially violent world. As a Croatian now living in the US, he has experienced disturbing and intense interrogation because of his identity. He describes how in the former Yugoslavia in 1983–4 he was summoned for national service and because of his marriage to an American woman and study of theology was considered a potential spy (Volf, 2006: 21). This resulted in several months of abusive threats and questioning, gross invasion of privacy and an overwhelming sense of fear (Volf, 2006: 53).

His most influential and award-winning work, *Exclusion and Embrace* (1996) is a sustained theological reflection on the implications of the theology of forgiveness and reconciliation against the backdrop of the wars in the former Yugoslavia, stimulated by the theologian Jurgen Moltmann's question to him in a lecture, 'but could you embrace a *cetnik* [violent Serbian fighter]?' (Volf, 1996: Preface). Social identity, he argues, should not be about rejecting the other as in the Kristevan analysis of identity construction, but about *embracing* the other. This is not simply a theoretical argument but is important for peace, justice and reconciliation in a bloody world.

Volf regards Christian cultural identity as dual: Christians belong to God's kingdom as well as their own nationality. No culture is more Christian than any other as all the peoples of the world, theoretically at least, have access to God and the potential to inculturate Christian belief within their own context (45). For the Christian, God's kingdom will always have primacy over national and cultural identity (40).

However, this dual identity is not dualistic. Volf sees culture not as separate from a Christian identity but as 'a space in which one lives, the air one breathes' (Volf, 2011: 90). Christians infuse their culture with meaning, and Volf uses the example of language as one method by which culture can be 'transformed from within' (91), for example when Christians use the same language as everyone else but words such as 'God' or 'marriage' have a new and different meaning for them (92). The task of Christians is not to see the Church and the world as different cultures, but to transform their own culture from the inside (92) and to be a positive rather than a reactive influence (95). He refers to it as 'to divert without leaving' one's own context (93).

The challenge for the Christian is to love God and neighbour (73) and put that faith into practice (72, 76), but often the Christian faith has 'malfunctioned' (3) and Christians have failed to live up to Christianity's prophetic nature, or have even been a destructive force:

> Too often [faith] … neither mends the world nor helps human beings thrive. To the contrary, it seems to shatter things into pieces, to choke up what is new and beautiful before it has a chance to take root, to trample underfoot what is good and true. When this happens, faith is no longer a spring of fresh water helping good life to grow lushly, but a poisoned well, more harmful to those who drink its waters than any single vice could be. (3)

He acknowledges that a 'thin' version of the faith speaks the language of Christianity but is utilised, subconsciously or unconsciously, to promote other ends (9). An extreme example of this is his description of the Serbian soldier riding a tank holding three fingers triumphantly in the air (the symbol of the Trinity), as a sign of his 'right' belief and therefore having the 'right' identity (18). Here, the malfunction of religion happens when the language and practices of faith are used to construct a social identity in an exclusionary (and violent) way, although Volf does not explore this comprehensively as he is writing from the perspective of the desirability of people of faith affecting culture.

There is no thorough examination of the corollary of this in his work, whereby cultures have appropriated religious practices and language and invested them with other meanings. There is an implication in his writings however that although the Christian faith challenges adherents to infuse culture with the

Christian faith, sometimes, as in the case of the Serbian tank driver, the Christian faith can be infused with practices which do not promote human flourishing, neither loving God nor loving our neighbour as ourselves (Volf, 2011: 9).

A clear example of faith leading to disempowerment rather than flourishing is in the discussions about identity within feminist theology, to which I now turn.

Tyranny of kind and nice

Several decades ago, Saiving Goldstein (1960) wrote an influential article arguing that women's 'sin' was not pride but rather the underdevelopment or negation of the self. Gill-Austern (1996: 304) developed this further, maintaining that Christian teaching about relationships, especially love as self-sacrifice and self-denial, has been particularly dangerous to women's psychological, emotional and physical health. She argues that women's identity is defined and developed in connection with others; however, this runs the risk of the individual woman losing 'herself' by finding meaning and self-esteem within relationships, sacrificing her sense of self in order to nurture others and maintain emotional bonds.

Women's style of relating to others can be characterised as 'the tyranny of kind and nice' (Gilligan in Gill-Austern, 1996: 306). The implications of women developing their identity in connection to others rather than in separation from them and running the risk of being overwhelmed by the needs of others is starkly described by Gill-Austern as the 'unholy trinity of self-abnegation, self-doubt and false guilt' (Gill-Austern, 1996: 307). A loss of a sense of self can lead to a form of depression that has arguably been a particular manifestation in women (Dunlap, 1997: 52). Another way of talking about this 'loss of self' is that of (self-) silencing (Dunlap, 1997: 52).

Research by Bons-Storm (1996) about the experience of women in church and of pastoral care showed that women felt silenced and that their pastoral concerns were ignored by the Church and its leaders. This was not just because women wanted to discuss issues that were considered unspeakable by the Church (and particularly male clergy) such as sexuality and domestic violence, but also because they felt ashamed of their emotions which they regarded as unacceptable within a male-led Church (Bons-Storm, 1996: 20). Bons-Storm's participants did not feel able to admit their ambivalence about motherhood, or to be honest about other negative emotions which would risk characterising them as selfish or controlling and therefore not a faithful Christian female disciple (Bons-Storm, 1996: 18). Bons-Storm's work has made an impact on feminist pastoral theology because the experiences recorded in the case studies (from the Netherlands) seemed to articulate the experiences of women elsewhere who have also felt devalued and ignored by clergy and the Church.

Problematising the connected self

And yet, valuing connection as a way of being for women is possibly more complex than the approach outlined above would suggest. As Fisk argues, the debate about connectedness, the self, autonomy and empowerment is a 'delicate balance' (Fisk, 2014: 85). On the one hand, it is important to acknowledge and appreciate the connectedness many women bring to relationships and relating as this reveals an important aspect of life and experience, something which is often socialised out of men (80). However, is it simply a matter of encouraging women to be more selfish rather than selfless and to speak rather than remain silent? Fisk suggests that feminist theology has not engaged deeply enough with the complexities of the issues raised by Saiving Goldstein for the interpersonal and everyday lives of women, moving too quickly to issues of structural injustice and neglecting the importance of the experience of relating as a self to others (Fisk, 2014: 85). She writes:

> Very often, my 'sins' are what Saiving calls 'feminine' ones and the realization of this has come as a surprise to me. I have always seen myself as rather independent, proud, assertive and not at all lacking in 'personality.' But I also recognize that, for all my feminist principles, I tend to see myself through the eyes of others. I forget that other people are not me. I often want to smooth things over; I go along with things. I find myself saying too much, spilling out, not respecting others' boundaries or my own. I desperately want union with others and this often results in me losing myself. With family, friends and lovers, I often struggle to distinguish their pain from my own; to separate my memories and narratives of the past from those of the people I love. (Fisk, 2014: 86)

I can identify with Fisk in that my own struggles with self-confidence, despite my poem 'Silences' in the introduction, are more complex than feeling 'silenced' or that my self has been overwhelmed by the needs of my family, friends, parishioners and colleagues. It is also difficult to work out what kind of self to enact in different situations. In order to express this I wrote the following poem using the metaphor of tea:

STEWED TEA

> Whenever tea is offered, I take it.
> It's bound to be better than the tea
> I make. I have it weak, so I make it
> too strong. Swirling the bag, again,
> again. So no one likes it. They ask
> for water instead. But I take their tea.
> Always.[4]

In this poem I convey the difficulty of trying to express myself in a way that is acceptable to others, that does not overcompensate for a lack of confidence by being too forceful. However, it also articulates a frustration at having to accept the strong views and feelings of others, whilst my own views and how they are expressed feels unacceptable.

Although Western feminist theologians have described women as having a disempowered and silenced identity especially within church life, Fisk's work (2014) indicates a more complex situation. The relationship between connectedness, the self, autonomy and empowerment for women affected by Christian traditions, institutions and teaching still requires further deep reflection. Is this also the situation in Wales – do Welsh women feel disempowered and silenced because of the teachings and practices of the Church?

In this chapter I have explored different theoretical approaches to identity that form the backdrop to this exploration. Both Butler and Kristeva argue for a constructivist understanding which sees identity as created and recreated in action and language. There is no essentialised 'real me' behind what I do and say, I become who I am in what I do and say. Because identity is not static or boundaried we cannot predict someone's characteristics based on their social identity. (Not all Welsh people can sing.) This more flexible approach to identity leads to freedom from prescribed roles, behaviours or characteristics and, ultimately, from the power of othering and stigmatisation.

As we have seen, identity has political implications, and can be constructed for political reasons. Volf's work has also shown how national identities can abuse religious language and practices in order to construct a damaging social identity. Feminist theologians have reminded us how Christian teaching on identity can contribute to the disempowerment and silencing of women. But even if our identities are developing and changing and cannot be easily defined, what remains are the stories we tell about ourselves, as individuals and as nations.

2

Constructed Welsh Identities?

Wales is an artefact which the Welsh produce; the Welsh make and remake Wales day by day and year after year. If they want to. (Williams, 1982: 200)

If identities are constructed in discourse and practice, are not stable but fluid, and if essentialised and boundaried identities have the potential for stigmatisation and even violence, is it possible or even desirable to speak of a distinctively Welsh identity or identities? Political leaders have deliberately spoken of Welshness in inclusive terms; for example Lord Ellis-Thomas, speaking about devolution, said that:

... the Assembly is about creating a notion of citizenship of Wales. That citizenship is open to everybody who chooses to be here. It doesn't matter where you come from. It doesn't matter what language you speak. (Giudici, 2012: 231)

I would also define Welsh identity as encompassing everyone who lives in Wales who wants to define themselves as Welsh (or partly Welsh), as opposed to a definition based on ethnicity (if that is possible) or language.

Theorists working in Wales as well as further afield also consider (national) identity to be formed in language and everyday action, and take a constructivist approach (Day, 2002: 230; Wodak, De Cillia, Reisigl and Liebhart, 2009: 2). They also recognise that nationality seems 'real' for most people in Wales, who have an unquestioning and unproblematic view of Wales as a bounded nation with its own history and artefacts (Day, 2002: 231). There is however tension between a view of identity as performed and evolving and discourses of identity which may themselves reflect reified and static thinking. In fact, nationalism by its very nature tends towards a monolithic understanding and interpretation of a nation, its story, national characteristics and cultural objects in order to unify a people (Day, 2002: 241).

National identity is performed not only within institutions, politics and in the public square, but also in everyday spaces such as the school gate, local shops, or in the media; there are also power implications as well as status and other forms of social capital to be lost or gained – we can gain or lose status in our everyday lives according to how Welsh (or any other national identity) we are (Day, 2002: 241). It is therefore uncontroversial to regard national identity as being performed within language and behaviours, and constantly evolving. It is important however to acknowledge that nationalism and national identity are problematic terms. One theoretical lens which recognises the evolving rather than static nature of national identity is seeing it as an 'imagined community' (Anderson, 2006).

An imagined community

For Anderson (2006), a nation is an imagined political community, where people adhere to a boundary and a set of characteristics and artefacts in their own imaginations along with a strong sense of belonging to a group of people and to territory. It is 'imagined' because as soon as a grouping exists beyond what is possible in face-to-face interactions it becomes an entity that is beyond the actual and real (Anderson, 2006: 6). There is a form to this community beyond physicality and boundaries, including particular characteristics and styles that are always developing. This imagined political community has enormous power in the lives of its adherents, leading them, as Anderson suggests, 'not so much to kill, as willingly to die for such limited imaginings' (Anderson, 2006: 7). If a nation demands allegiance, even to the point of death (as was seen in the world wars in the last century and violence in this century), in most cases this loyalty is freely given. The imagined community of a nation is highly potent in individual lives.

An imagined community is similar to the concepts outlined by other theorists who have attempted to describe a whole social world with its own norms, values and practices. Brockmeier describes this helpfully:

> Geertz's (1983) idea of 'common sense as a cultural system', Bruner's (1990) notion of 'folk psychology', Foucault's (1966/1970) concept of 'episteme' and Bourdieu's (1980/1990) conception of 'habitus' suggest consonant visions. What binds individuals together into a cultural community is the centripetal force of a connective structure that organizes a considerate body of thought and knowledge, beliefs and concepts of self: that is, a worldview rooted in a set of social rules and values as well as in the shared memory and of a commonly inhabited and similarly experienced past. (Brockmeier 2002: 18)

Also similar to 'imagined world' is Gee's concept of a 'figured world' which is created (or emerges) in discourse (Gee, 2011: 70). The sense that Welshness is an imagined community is a helpful way of understanding Welsh identity and the part religion plays in its construction in that it points to common assumptions, practices and language which can be identified and then examined.

Anderson's 'imagined community' is less helpful than other concepts such as 'figured worlds' as he assumes that religion is a separate imagined community from a national identity. For example, he argues that the rise of nationality came through the waning of the influence of other dominant ideologies such as religion (Anderson, 2006: 22). This contradicts the work of Martin (2014) who argues that far from nationalism superseding religion as secularism becomes more entrenched, both nationalism and secularism are, in fact, similar in terms of concepts and dynamic and have the same foundational potential pull towards boundaries and the potential for violence precisely because they bind people together (Martin, 2014: 991).

In the case of Wales, as I argue later in the book, the role of Nonconformism has been historically significant in creating a distinctive Welsh identity and plays an important part in the creation of this imagined community. We cannot distinguish religion from nationhood, although Anderson regards narratives (2006:

208) and language (2006: 46) as important aspects of nationality, despite neglecting religion.

In addition to Anderson's description of nationhood as a mental construct of an imagined community, Wodak, De Cillia, Reisigl and Liebhart (2009) propose further theoretical bases from which to look at nationality which again locate it within discourse. They see it as a special form of social identity, which is 'produced and reproduced as well as transformed and dismantled discursively' (4). They also regard national identity as a set of emotional temperaments, attitudes and behavioural conventions which are internalised through socialisation and which contains an emphasis on inter-national distinctiveness whilst tending to ignore intra-national differences. They also maintain that national identities are non-essentialist and that they are 'malleable, fragile and frequently, ambivalent and diffuse' (4). For them, national identity is inclusive of both cultural and political concepts (4).

Their framework shows that it is possible to hold a view of national identity which is non-essentialist, but in which we are able to explore certain practices, behaviours, emotional dispositions and forms of language which alert us to what are considered to be the features of this identity at a particular point in time. There are dangers inherent in this, particularly in reifying any aspect of nationality and the resulting danger of stigmatisation from stereotyping. However, it is important to accept that national identity is not static and that stereotyping, although 'real' in discourse, does not convey the complexity of human personal and social identity.

If Wales is an imagined community, created and maintained within discourse, what are the elements and characteristics of this identity? Before looking at the role religion has played in developing Welsh myths and stereotypes I want to look first at an ethnographic work which sought to describe Welsh attributes and then discuss whether Welsh identity is a postcolonial identity.

Welsh identity performed

There is a danger of essentialising Welsh people in discussions about characteristics; however research by Trosset (1993) has attempted to describe the features that appear within Welsh discourses of identity, and her work is interesting as well as useful. Although this study has been critiqued for its concentration on a particular stratum of Welsh culture, that of a highly educated, Welsh-speaking middle-class clique (Morris, 1995: 333), the work helpfully identifies characteristics that Welsh people themselves regard as being 'Welsh', which she found to be 'hegemonic ... but not uncontested' (Trosset and Caulkins, 2001: 68). Her work shows that it is possible to research national characteristics and assumptions within everyday discourse and behaviours.

Although she is aware of the dangers of essentialising certain Welsh attributes (she would also claim to have a constructivist approach to identity) (Trosset, 1993: 4), she maintains that she has identified certain qualities which are recognisable within discourses of Welshness, with which Welsh people themselves identify

(5). For her, identity is 'performative' (that is, constructed in action, behaviours and language) and not essential:

> Ethnicity, then, in a theoretical sense, is not an essence but a discourse. It is not, however, just a discourse, an idea ungrounded in 'real life'. Ethnicity is a discourse about something real and it is also an experience of the subject of discourse. (51)

This discourse of Welshness, as well as its performance, has an impact on the emotional lives of Trosset's research participants and particularly so when related to stratification, which she argues is on the basis of 'Welshness'. Highly regarded people are honoured for 'exemplary Welshness' but the corollary of this is that there are others in Wales who are lower down on the hierarchy, who feel 'shame' and 'alienation' rather than 'pride' or 'affinity' (55):

> There is a prestige system in Wales based on this principle, one in which people are honoured for the committed performance of ethnically relevant activities and for their demonstrated skill at these pursuits. These people include eisteddfod winners, adjudicators and officials, language teachers and scholars, chapel ministers, individuals who are unusually knowledgeable about Welsh history and traditions, nationalist politicians and leaders of ethnically-conscious organisations and exceptionally skilled practitioners of 'traditionally Welsh' agricultural pursuits … (55)

In discussing status Trosset also refers to work by Frankenberg and Emmet on the reluctance Welsh people show to claim positions of power or authority for themselves; apparently 'it is not Welsh to put yourself forward' (85). This also has an effect on agency: Trosset maintains that positions of influence are awarded rather than gained, and are considered therefore to be 'unattainable' (89).

Although she does not discuss gender at any great length, she makes some pertinent observations (though unsubstantiated with direct quotes or scenarios) about women and emotions, claiming that expected gender responses are somehow reversed. This deserves further research and exploration. She writes:

> It is not … the case that people are more familiar within their own gender: there is a tendency for women to be more formal whether they are interacting with other women or with men. This fits in with one Welsh man's characterization of men as generally 'less refined'. I was consistently struck by the impression that men, in public social settings were much more relaxed, warm and casual while women were more formal, withdrawn and impersonal and less expressive of emotion. (105)

Another interesting aspect of Trosset's work is her exploration of power and control. She refers to the concept of the 'strong character' and also to the commonplace assertion of 'powerlessness' (121), with people sometimes competing to present themselves as having a lower status than others and 'modesty' or 'equality' being highly prized values in an individual (122). Having power (or presumably confidence) to influence the world is seen as an 'English' characteristic. According to Trosset, two British immigrant Welsh-learners told her 'that most people would rather sit and stew about things rather than doing something constructive to change them' (123); Trosset also asserts that many Welsh people consider themselves as a 'conquered nation' (124) and as such believe that they are stigmatised (125).

Two characteristics that seem to contradict one another are what Trosset refers to as performativity and emotionalism. On the one hand the Welsh people in her study seem to make a strong distinction between public and private behaviour. Public behaviour is very 'controlled' to the extent that negative and private emotions remain hidden, out of politeness (129). However, Welsh people are also outwardly emotional, effusive and tactile. As an American, she found the 'contrived' nature of Welsh behaviour unnerving in the sense that she could never be sure of how people she did not know very well were actually feeling. Her own experience of 'Americanness' is that there is a much stronger correlation between actions and inner thoughts and feelings (146). My experience visiting the US was that the 'have a nice day' culture seems similarly contrived to Welsh people.

Goffman's work on identity and role is pertinent to Trosset's discussion of how Welshness is 'performed' in social spaces such as the home. Goffman argues that people assume roles and 'perform' them by managing carefully the impression they give to others about themselves, in much the same way as actors perform characters in a play (Goffman, 1959: Preface). He usefully explores this as a 'back region', where access to others is controlled and the performance prepared, and the 'front region' where the performance is executed (231). The idea of performance and a front and back region is particularly important in Welsh notions of respectability, as Trosset (1993) argues, and this is seen physically in the home with its front room or parlour and back room or even kitchen. If Trosset is right, Welsh concepts of the self have the idea of a respectable identity that is prepared in the 'back region' and performed in the 'front region' at their core.

She also considered Welsh behaviour to be 'exaggerated' (Trosset, 1993: 147). Yet 'artificiality' is a highly unacceptable characteristic amongst Welsh people – it is important for emotion to seem genuine. Trosset also speaks approvingly of the warm and physically intimate emotionalism of Welsh people, which she does not consider to be part of this performativity. Nostalgia (conveyed by the uniquely Welsh word for longing, *hiraeth)* is also characteristic of Welsh people in her study. Interestingly, experiencing and expressing strong emotions seems more notable in men than women (Trosset, 1993: 154), whilst everyone is expected to become personally involved and engaged with people and issues; disengagement and distance are frowned upon.

According to Trosset, the characteristic Welsh assumptions are:

1. *Egalitarianism* – that all people are equal and that relationships are based on the connection between people rather than 'status roles'. An example of this is how someone will be introduced not by what they do, but who they are in relation to others.
2. *Martyrdom* – self-sacrifice on behalf of the group is highly prized.
3. *Emotionalism* – emotional engagement is expected and emotional detachment is seen as suspect. However, this view is held in parallel with the

belief that inner feelings do not and need not always match outward behaviour.

4. *Performance* – the acknowledgement that people are 'performers' and will behave very differently in public and in private. (Though Trosset does not make this explicit, this is also heavily linked to respectability.)
5. *Nostalgia* – a longing for the past and the feeling that something has been lost, expressed by the untranslatable Welsh word *hiraeth*. (Trosset and Caulkins, 2001: 66–8)

Although Trosset's research is only one ethnographer's experience of certain parts of Wales and is by now several decades old, the book is well written, reflexive and compelling, with some humorous and rich descriptions.[5] More direct quotes from participants would have further enriched her work, and although she has been criticised for essentialising the characteristics of Welsh people (Badone, 1995: 601), her findings have given me a depth of insight into my own culture and are an accurate portrayal of the values and assumptions of middle-class Welsh speakers in my experience.

Trosset's work has articulated for me a sense that stratification within Welsh identity is distinctive and occurs along 'Welshness' lines. A shop assistant who is a poet would have a higher status in this social world than the shop owner who is relatively uncultured. Her identification of a lack of confidence and agency within Welsh identity can be usefully explored by looking at postcolonialism and Welsh identity.

A postcolonial identity?

Economically and socially, Wales shares many of the privileges of other Western nations. However, there is an ongoing debate within Welsh studies as to whether it is accurate to call Wales postcolonial. Jones argues that Wales is postcolonial because of the continuing effect of an unequal relationship with England (Jones, 2005: 24), with Thomas maintaining that the language of colonisation has been present in discussions about devolution and pointing out that Conservative secretaries of state in the 1980s and 1990s were branded in derogatory terms as 'viceroys' (Thomas, 2005: 85). In fact John Redwood's political adviser, Hywel Williams, recommended to him a passage from E. M. Forster's *A Passage to India* as the best description of the Welsh relationship to the English:

> A subjugated race wished to please, and, in over-egging the pudding succeeded in annoying both the conquerors and in exacerbating its own latent self-disgust. (Thomas, 2005: 91)

It is possible to claim that Wales was the first colonised nation. Williams considers it 'plausible' to argue that since the death of the last prince of Wales Llywelyn ap Gruffydd in 1282, 'Wales [has] stood in something of a colonial relationship to England' (Williams, 2005: 5) and refers to Davies's (1974) exploration of the subjugation of Welsh people through intentional immigration and the occupation of important administrative posts by English men, with Welsh people being given inferior legal status and in some circumstances having their land seized (Williams, 2005: 4). The Acts of Union (1536 and 1543) gave equal legal status once more to Welsh men, although monoglot Welsh men were forbidden to hold high office; this was despite the fact, as Williams notes, that both the Prayer Book and Bible were in Welsh by this time. The effect of the Acts of Union was that Wales became part of an expanded England rather than a colony (Williams, 2005: 6). This administrative reality has been culturally as well as politically significant.

He concedes that 'cultural imperialism' in terms of the 'huge cultural presence' of England and the strength of the English language has led to the position of the Welsh language as 'precarious' (11). However, he considers it 'self-indulgent and potentially offensive' (10) to draw parallels between Wales and the experience of violence and subjugation of countries colonised in the nineteenth century, not least because Welsh people themselves took part in the colonisation and enslavement of other peoples.

Perhaps it is not as important to conclude the debate as to acknowledge the complexity with which Welsh identity and stigmatisation is regarded: a strand of postcolonial thought recognises the ambivalence and hybridity in postcolonial identity (Aaron and Williams, 2005: xvi). Thomas suggests persuasively that Wales has more in common with countries such as New Zealand, Australia and Ireland with a perceived inferiority and 'cultural cringe' as a mental rather than physical colonisation (Thomas, 2005: 86, 87). She states:

> Welsh political culture has historically had a self-image of dependence, seeing itself as too small or too poor to aspire to autonomy ... There has often been a mindset that Wales is 'too divided' or 'too parochial', which implies that Wales is ungovernable without the assertion of an outside authority. (Thomas, 2005: 96)

Wales could be said to have an 'image problem' recognised by Welsh people themselves (Pitchford, 2001). In fact Pitchford's research indicates that Welsh people do have an 'inferiority complex' and that colonisation (internal or otherwise) has lowered individuals' confidence (55). This image problem is complex in that other aspects of stereotyped Welsh identity can also be romanticised and even celebrated (55). They are certainly persistent, as I now explore particularly in relation to religion.

In this chapter I have explored Welshness as a constructed social identity. Anderson's work is useful here, describing national identity as an 'imagined community'. One ethnographer, Trosset, has outlined a possible set of characteristics identified in her research that are distinctively Welsh, especially within Wales's Welsh-speaking communities where modesty is prized and connections between people are more important than their status in society. Status can be earned according to how 'Welsh' one is in terms of paid and voluntary roles, hobbies, gifts and talents and expertise. Many Welsh people consider themselves as 'powerless' and part of this lack of agency is also reflected in perceptions that Wales is too small, and lacks the resources of its more powerful and confident neighbour. Even if Wales is not technically postcolonial, it certainly does suffer from 'cultural cringe'.

THEOLOGY SEMINAR

She forms her words
like mangoes in her mouth,
eyes unconvinced
she has the right to say
pedagogy, womanist,
pneumatology.
Though neither of us
need a dictionary,
we still glance
towards the man
in the beard and tie. (Ceridwen 2011b: 50)

3

Wales, Religion and Identity

The Welsh, in particular, have survived despite the lack of a separate legal and educational system and a recent history that has witnessed massive immigration and integrationist pressures ... The Welsh, nevertheless, are, in their contrasts and diversity, yma o hyd – 'still here'. (R. Merfyn Jones, 1992: 330)

The surprising feature of Welsh identity is that it is, as Jones suggests, 'still here'. He comments that 'English visitors' have come to Wales for the past two centuries on holiday, viewing Welsh people 'in a benign if patronizing fashion as an honest, industrious, pious people wedded to their mountains and to the Welsh language and its culture' (Jones, 1992: 331). These stereotypes about Wales and Welsh people, however, are not just historical or symbolic like Scottish bagpipes and kilts, or the English bowler hat: they form the daily expectations of many people visiting Wales.

Day (2002) recounts an astonishing story of how delegates at a British Sociological Association conference meeting in Aberystwyth in the 1980s surprised the conference organisers by asking if they could visit the 'local collieries' (Day, 2002: 2) whereas in fact the nearest coal mines were at least eighty miles away, probably a four-hour round trip in the car. Day comments:

These visitors were responding to an image of Wales in which the mental landscape was dominated by winding gear, the blackened faces of miners and doubtless some associated scenery of rugby football and male voice choirs. (Day, 2002: 2)

Although Day does not mention this, a significant part of the above image is normally a chapel building and it is argued that the characteristics of Welsh people have been formed in part by Wales's religious history, particularly Nonconformity and revivals, and that there are certain values that make Welsh people unique, such as a strong sense of belonging to a people and a place, a democratic ethos, tolerance and a lack of materialism (Day, 2002: 19).

It could be argued according to Castells's (2010) schema that this is a resistance identity, constructed in order to resist the dominant English forces by essentialising certain characteristics of Welsh people. A major aspect of this resistance identity is the pervasiveness of the perception of Wales being a Nonconformist country.

Welsh identities and Christianity in recent historical context

Dominance of the myth of Nonconformist Wales

It is virtually uncontested to say that Christianity, particularly Nonconformity, has had a strong influence on the ethos, values and habits of people living in Wales (Chambers and Thompson, 2005a: 337; Jones, 1992: 338; Phillips, 1997: 3). In his book about Welsh religion and art, Harvey regards the Free Churches as 'among the most powerful forces acting upon nineteenth- and early twentieth-century Wales' in their effect on every aspect of Welsh culture – politics, education and society in general (Harvey, 1995: 3). Chambers and Thompson state that 'Calvinistic Methodism' has occupied 'a pivotal role in the cultural and social history of Wales' particularly within identity formation (2005a: 338). This is part of a longer association between Christianity and Welsh identity. Morgan maintains that Christian identity and Welshness were 'so tightly intertwined as to be virtually indistinguishable', astonishingly, since the seventh century (1999: 327). The role of Nonconformity in Wales could be characterised as 'established dissidence' (Davie, 2015: 102).

The nature of this Nonconformist influence, however, is acknowledged to be at least ambivalent and can be characterised critically as a 'rigid public morality' (Chambers, 2005: 1). Trosset also argues that to be 'chapel' is to be regarded as more Welsh, and that those who feel less Welsh have a lesser status within Welsh culture, and a corresponding sense of shame and alienation (Trosset, 1993: 55). Therefore, this perception has had an effect not simply on the social identities of Welsh people, but on their ego identity too, how they think and feel about themselves.

The argument that religion plays a formative part in national identity and is inseparable from it is not distinctive to Wales. Pace argues that a promotion of the particular role of Catholicism in European national identity has been a 'core strategy of the Roman Catholic Church' (Pace, 2007: 43). Within the UK, Davie (1994: 14) argues that the denominations themselves have become 'carriers of cultural identity' in Scotland as well as Wales, and Day (2011) argues that being a Christian for many English people is a cultural rather than a religious identification. And yet, the pervasiveness of the role of Nonconformity in Wales remains.

A personal account of the impact of Nonconformity on Welsh identity, religion and culture is given by Llywelyn (1999). He explains that to be Welsh was to be 'chapel':

> As a child growing up in this ethnic Protestant Welsh religiosity, I equated Welshness with religiosity and righteousness. To worship God anywhere else other than in a chapel and in any language other than Welsh, was both alien and wrong – and that wrongness was as much a cultural as a religious sin. (Llywelyn, 1999: x)

Thomas argues that this is a *mythomoteur*, that is, a 'dynamic generative concept of identity, necessary for the emergence of a modern ethnie' (Thomas, 2010: 8, 9) which is surprising given that 'historians have emphasised that at no point, even at the very height of Nonconformist culture, did the majority of Welsh people attend chapel' (Thomas, 2010: 8). For Thomas, Nonconformity has been a significant (if not the only) aspect of this constructed resistance identity. Even if Thomas's claims that Nonconformity was never as dominant as the myth suggests are true, it certainly is not now. According to the 2011 census[6] the number of those calling themselves Christian has fallen dramatically from 71.9 per cent in 2001 to 57.6 per cent, making Wales less Christian than any region of England.

Whose Wales is it anyway?

If Morgan is right that 'from the outset, the Christian religion seemed to be part of the essence of Welshness' (Morgan, 1999: 1) it is debatable which type of Christianity has safeguarded Welsh identity the most. In fact all the denominations have at one stage or another laid claim to being heirs of the Celtic Church and to being the national church of Wales (Hughes, 2001: 123).

The safeguarding of Welsh identity, customs and language has been a continuous concern from the sixteenth century onwards, with eighteenth-century writers lamenting the decline of the Welsh way of life and commenting that 'the Welsh were becoming like the English' (Morgan, 1983: 43). This originated in the sixteenth century with the eradication of the native legal system, the weakening of the bardic system and the outlawing of the Welsh language within public administration (Morgan, 1983: 44). The language seemed to be in danger in the seventeenth century, with Huw Hughes writing in a letter to Lewis Morris in 1730 that 'all the defenders of the old language had gone to sleep' (Morgan, 1983: 44). In 1729 John Roderick wrote to Lewis Morris to complain that he could not find anyone who could understand the instructions in the manuscripts for Welsh traditional music (Morgan, 1983: 50).

The practices that had been bound up with Catholicism were also one of the losses in cultural terms in the sixteenth century (Morgan, 1983: 44), and, in the eighteenth century, the effect of the Methodist revival was to diminish traditions such as saints' days, patronal festivals and fairs and a social life which revolved around drink, church, sports and dancing:

> Elias Owen the great folklorist in his fascinating book on the old stone crosses of the Vale of Clwyd shows how Victorian church restoration removed stairways connecting the chancels to local taverns, removed niches kept in the Churches for the prize ale given by the parson to winners in the Sunday sports, removed ball courts from the churchyards, and placed huge marble graves in churchyards formerly laid out for dances and sports meetings. All this would be of interest to folklorists only if it were not for the fact that the common people whose lives were now totally transformed were also the last repositories of Welsh lore, music, historical learning, poetry and language. The changes in folk life had a fundamental importance in the eyes of scholars and patriots, who saw that if Wales were to survive at all, it would have to find some new artificial supports. (Morgan, 1983: 54–5)

The 'artificial supports' created following on from the Methodist Revival to sustain and reinvigorate Welsh identity, traditions and customs, to supersede the more worldly (albeit equally Welsh customs) of drinking, dancing and sports, remain to this day as significant aspects of Welsh life, particularly the eisteddfod.

Meetings of bardic associations had been recorded as early as 1176 and were revived in 1700 (Morgan, 1983: 56–7); the turning point came in 1819 where at the Carmarthen Eisteddfod the Gorsedd of the Bards was first introduced into what had earlier been simply musical and literary competitions (Morgan, 1983: 60). The Gorseddau, along with other eisteddfodic rituals, were created by Edward Williams (known by his bardic name as Iolo Morganwg) who maintained that the Welsh bards were inheritors of the ancient Druids in an apostolic succession and created the rituals based on his own reading of folklore and his Unitarian faith as well as his own imagination (Morgan, 1983: 60).

Along with a renewed interest in Celtic mythology and early Celtic Christianity, this gave Wales a separate mythological history from England (Morgan, 1983: 68). Individual leaders such as Morganwg, and social and cultural trends, along with religious and nationalistic movements, helped promote or diminish practices and customs which were an important part of Welsh identity in accordance with their own beliefs and commitments at the time.

The constructed identity which utilised Nonconformity arguably had a detrimental effect on older Welsh traditions and beliefs, and was deliberately constructed. Morgan argues that a new and enduring identity emerged in the eighteenth century, with its own traditions and culture:

> The Nonconformist takeover of Welsh culture created a new image. It weakened Welsh interest in the far-distant national past, replacing it with an interest in the past of the Old Testament and with the early history of dissenting causes in the seventeenth and eighteenth centuries and emphasized the new puritanical Sunday as 'The Welsh Sunday', the new 'Welsh way of life' being that of the chapel, the singing school (for hymns not ballads), the temperance assemblies, the Cymanfa Ganu (hymn singing assemblies), the quarterly meetings and associations, the mutual improvement societies and much else which is familiar to the twentieth century as the typical Wales. (Morgan, 1983: 95)

The role of Nonconformity in constructing this 'typical Wales' is beginning to be evaluated and reappraised. Brooks (2015) for example argues that its Calvinistic (and therefore fatalistic) outlook and focus on the world to come led ironically to an unquestioning and obedient attitude towards England's domination of Wales (38) and to the sacrifice of the language on the altar of a constructed religious identity (135).

Brooks questions the narrative of Nonconformity having empowered the Welsh *gwerin* (working class or 'commoners') of the nineteenth century in the face of oppression from Toryism and the Anglican Church, commenting that a discourse of the Church in Wales (and Conservative politics) as the enemy of a confident Welsh identity is still operative in the lives of Welsh people today (Brooks, 2015: 49). The Church in Wales (or the Church of England as it was before 1920 and disestablishment) was known as both *Yr Hen Fam* (the old mother) and *Yr Hen Estrones* (the old stranger) and, therefore, even more contested than evaluating the role of Nonconformity is the role and influence of the Church in Wales within Wales, a discourse which is still influential in Welsh life.

As an Anglican priest, I am not in the best position to be objective about my own denomination. However my experience has been that despite conducting my ministry through the medium of Welsh (particularly when I worked in the Ogwen valley) and knowing the strong commitment to the language and culture amongst some of my colleagues within the Church in Wales, the discourse of the Anglican Church as enemy or oppressor is still salient.

Through researching the historical context of religion and Welsh identity I realised that the history of Anglicanism and Welsh identity is ambivalent, and different from the narrative of the Anglican Church as the enemy of the *gwerin* and of a confident Welsh identity, of monoglot clergy and bishops unsympathetic to both their people and their language. The role played by Bishop William Morgan in translating the Bible into Welsh in 1588 is credited with preserving the language, and just over a century later, the role of Griffith Jones, Rector of Llanddowror and his circulating schools in raising literacy and educational levels in Wales cannot be underestimated. Various commentators (including Brooks, 2015) also point to the influence of the group of Anglican clergy known as the *Hen Bersoniaid Llengar* (The Old Literary Parsons) who were crucial in the development of the eisteddfodic customs, in the preservation of Welsh traditions, manuscripts and other writings, in promoting the language within the Anglican Church, in Wales and in their condemnation of the appointment of monoglot English-speaking clergy and bishops (Jones, 1963: 6, 7).

More recently, in the twentieth century, disestablishment ironically helped the Church in Wales to flourish (relatively speaking) by reclaiming a Welsh identity, due, in part, to the appointment of Welsh speakers to key positions, including Dr Maurice Jones as principal at St David's College, Lampeter and a succession of Welsh-speaking bishops such as Timothy Rees, J. C. Jones, Glyn Simon and G. O. Williams (Morgan, 1999: 334, 337).

The conversion of the dramatist, activist and influential nationalist politician Saunders Lewis to Roman Catholicism also played a part in breaking the bond between Welsh identity and Nonconformity (Morgan, 1999: 335). Furthermore, 'chapel' culture began to be seen as repressive and increasingly out of tune with people's aspirations and lives:

> Whereas chapel religion was seen to be oppressive and puritanical, Anglicanism, with its Prayer Book liturgy, sacramentalism and rounded doctrines of creation and incarnation, provided a very appealing version of Christian faith. Unencumbered by the negativities of sabbatarianism and teetotalism, it presented a viable spiritual alternative for those who were offended by Nonconformity but chose not to succumb to secularism and irreligion. Not a few of its most distinguished lay members and senior clerics were former Nonconformists. Yet perhaps the most interesting contemporary development involved the change of attitude within the Church to Welsh nationality and identity. (Morgan, 1999: 337)

The Anglican Church came to be seen as a more positive and life-affirming institution, which meant that those who wished to reject the strictness of Nonconformity but still wanted to remain Christians found in the Anglican Church a new spiritual home, made possible by the Church in Wales's relatively recent embracing of Welsh identity (Morgan, 1999: 337). It is now the largest Christian denomination in Wales (Chambers and Thompson, 2005a: 342), whereas the

Nonconformist denominations are experiencing drastic decline (Chambers and Thompson, 2005b: 29, 30) which could be said to date from the years immediately following the Revival of 1904 (Roberts, 2013: 449).

In reality the Revival was short-lived, with a significant drop in numbers occurring soon afterwards (Roberts, 2013: 136) due to people losing interest and in some cases being excommunicated for alcohol and other issues (Roberts, 2013: 256). However, comments surrounding the Revival itself also show that Wales, even at the turn of the century, still had a conflicting and complex relationship with so called 'chapel culture' and its enforcement of rigid morality.

For example, one writer commented in the Welsh radical journal *Y Cronicl* in 1906 that:

> ... the eisteddfod was a festival of literature and drink and in recent years the smell of alcohol was upon it. We are thankful for a Revival that has turned a drunken eisteddfod into a sober eisteddfod. (Roberts, 2013: 85)

The influence of Nonconformity on Welsh identity and culture, then, was uneven in the latter part of the nineteenth century and had begun to wane by the beginning of the twentieth. It is now in crisis in the twenty-first century, as I now explore.

Secularism, religion and identity in Britain and in Wales

The results of the 2011 census

Despite the dominance of the perception of Wales as a religious nation, the 2011 census revealed that it is, in fact, more secular than any English region, and between 2001 and 2011 the percentage of the population of Wales who identified as Christian fell dramatically from 71.9 to 57.6 per cent.[7] During that time, the percentage of the population who claimed no religion increased by nearly half a million, from 18.5 to 32.1 per cent. Some areas in Wales reported the highest levels of no religion, for example Caerphilly, with 41 per cent claiming no religious affiliation whatsoever (Office for National Statistics 2012: 7). Although the census figures do not break down the figures by religious denomination, it can no longer be said that Christianity, let alone Nonconformism, has the overwhelming allegiance of people in Wales.

Across the regions of England and Wales, Wales is also the least ethnically diverse area with 95.65 per cent identifying as white. Minority ethnic groups are concentrated in the south and in urban areas. Nearly two thirds (66 per cent) described their identity as Welsh, a category that could be chosen alongside others, for example British. The highest proportion of self-identified Christians was found in the northern counties of Flintshire, Anglesey, Conwy and Denbighshire.

Despite the dramatic fall in numbers, Christianity is still the largest religion with 57.6 per cent. The nearest, Islam, only has 1.5 per cent of the population as adherents. In terms of religion, as well as ethnicity, Wales is relatively monochrome. The small percentages of other faiths translate into tiny numbers: for example in my own county of Conwy there are (according to the census) only 17 Sikhs, 206 Hindus, 62 Jews, 583 Muslims and 347 Buddhists. The population of Wales is overwhelmingly Christian (albeit not regularly attending churches) or non-religious. However, this loose Christian affiliation is falling at a significant rate.

Secularisation and modernity

In the literature on secularism, only scant attention is given to the different histories and cultures of the different nations within the UK.[8] The exception is Davie, who acknowledges the differences, albeit briefly (Davie, 1994: 3). Classically, secularisation theory has argued that modernity would ultimately lead increasingly towards irreligiosity and correspondingly to a gradual and permanent decline in numbers attending churches (Warner, 2010: 253–358).

This has led to the analysis that we are now facing the 'death of Christian Britain' in that we can no longer expect Christianity to 'confer' a certain kind of cultural identity on the British people (Brown, 2001: 193). This is ascribed to the changing role of women since the sexual revolution of the 1960s (Brown, 2001) or, more generally, to the irrelevance of the Christian church to younger generations, their indifference and adherence to cultural relativism (Bruce, 2002: 117, 240), or to the subjective 'turn' in the West and the resulting effect of a more individualistic and postmodern approach to spirituality (Heelas and Woodhead, 2005). That there are serious attempts to trace the genealogies of thought and culture, and to analyse them in relation to religious trends and apply them, indicates that secularisation as a response to modernity is more complex than the secularisation theory suggests.

Davie argues for a nuanced and complex understanding of the interplay between religious influences in public life, in personal faith and in church attendance, leading her to characterise the British situation as the predominance of 'believing without belonging' (Davie, 1994).[9] This phrase has been widely disseminated and adopted and seems to have provided some comfort to church leaders facing this decline. However others have argued that the affiliation to Christianity is more to do with believing 'in' belonging; an affiliation to (a British national) identity rather than a set of beliefs (Day, 2011).

English and Welsh national identities

As we have seen, religion has been interpreted as an important marker of Welsh identity (Morgan, 1999: 1). However Day (2011) argues that Christianity is also a carrier of national identity for English people, although this is not linked to denomination and is often related to white ethnicity. It can also represent a rejection of multiculturalism and a pride in an Englishness which can be exclusive and sometimes racist. She has categorised this Christian identity in three ways: 'natal' (because it is about baptism and family); 'ethnic' (because about culture and country) and 'aspirational' (because being Christian is being good).[10]

This is qualitatively different from the Welsh identification with Nonconformity, even though there are some parallels in that this identity has also been developed against a perceived threat – not multiculturalism but a dominant and oppressive English identity (Chambers, 2003: 125). It would also be naive to think that Wales is a 'tolerant nation' free from prejudice and racial tension, or that racism is simply an English incomer phenomenon in Wales (Williams, 2003: 220). A 'mythology' of tolerance and a positive attitude towards multiculturalism is one element in a constructed Welsh identity, sometimes in opposition to an English identity which is seen as 'imperialist and domineering' (Williams, Evans and O'Leary, 2003: 4). However the largest ethnic minority in Wales is people who come from England, and, therefore, debates about race, language and immigration are framed very differently. In fact, the Commission for Racial Equality and race equality councils have reported complaints of racism from those of English origin (Williams, 2003: 223).

Wales and secularism

Writing in 2005, Chambers and Thompson argue that secularisation has 'bitten deeper and harder' in Wales than anywhere else in Britain (Chambers and Thompson, 2005a: 338). The denominations most identified with Welsh identity, the Free Churches, have been hardest hit. In fact, Chambers notes that the decline is so marked that he predicted that only 2 per cent of chapels built in the late nineteenth century would still be open in twenty years' time (Chambers, 2005b: 20). The denomination that is most characteristically Welsh, the (Calvinistic Methodist) Presbyterian Church of Wales, had only sixty-four full-time ministers in 2005. This is a smaller number than most Church in Wales dioceses (Chambers 2005b: 21). In 2015 there were forty-five ministers working full-time for the Presbyterian Church in Wales,[11] and for the (Anglican) Church in Wales there were 445.[12] Although all the traditional denominations are declining, the largest denominations in Wales are the Anglican and the Catholic churches (Davie, 2015: 102).

Chambers argues that Welsh culture is 'post Christian' (Chambers, 2008: 87); however, he notes that the religious history of Wales is not the trajectory of decline that secularisation theory would predict. He quotes Lewis Morris who said that religion was 'quite out of taste, it is such an old fashioned thing', noting ironically that the quote is from 1757 (Chambers, 2008: 86). From the mid-eighteenth century on, religion in Wales underwent a dramatic transformation during the Methodist Revival and subsequently in the revivals of the early twentieth century. These came on the back of industrialisation and great social change and, as Chambers comments, 'religion in Wales was clearly waxing at a time when, according to the [secularism] paradigm, it should have been waning' (Chambers, 2011: 274).

There are four factors which characterise the particular Welsh experience of secularisation according to Chambers. They are the Welsh language and its decline, the professionalisation of ministry and a corresponding alienation of the working classes, the particular rural and industrial economic context and the rise of the welfare state (Chambers, 2011: 274, 275).

While this economic context was not unique to Wales, issues to do with language and identity were clearly significant and unparalleled, and Chambers's point about the emerging divisions between a middle-class religious elite and an alienated working-class membership merits further reflection. The particular egalitarian nature of Welsh society, as argued by Trosset (or rather the perception of it as such by many Welsh people) and the different forms of social capital and belonging that exist to varying degrees in Wales are a different sort of seedbed for religion and faith.

Chambers (2005) considers the activity of faith groups in social action as a 'turning point' and as a way in which the Church is gaining influence. Churches have found a voice in society, albeit 'comparatively muted' (348), mainly through the creation of the National Assembly Government which has given opportunities for faith groups to get involved in issues of national and public importance such as debt and rural poverty (349). The liaison officer for CYTUN (Churches Together in Wales, an ecumenical grouping) argued that this was a new form of Christianity:

> Formal religion is in decline. But what I think I will say is that the Christian faith in particular is still very much alive and kicking but it has to find a different way of being a Church. And this is one of the things that we found, for example, in my role, although it's not per se a converting role or a faith role in that sense, but it does actually bring church into the far corners of a secular and political world ... it's simply a new way of being a Church in a secular context. (Chambers and Thompson, 2005b: 36)

Bruce (2010) describes this dramatic downturn in church and chapel-going in a study of four rural northern Welsh villages, comparing them to earlier studies. The Christian tradition was seen as hegemonic in 1940 with almost all villagers belonging to church or chapel, unless they were 'English incomers'. For example one Croesor inhabitant said: 'The people down in Llanfrothen might have been a bit less religious because there were more English incomers there' (Bruce, 2010: 223). The decline in Llanfihangel, meanwhile, was described as moving from a situation in 1940 where 'almost everyone' had church or chapel affiliation, with half attending services, to only a third who were members of a Christian institution and only a sixth regularly worshipping (Bruce, 2010: 229).

The changes Bruce notes between 1950 and 2007, as well as a marked decline in church and chapel affiliation and attendance, are the disappearance of sabbatarianism, the death of Sunday schools, transformation in attitudes to drink (he notes that teetotalism is only referred to now in humour), a lack of interest in theological disputes,[13] a 'club' mentality and inward-lookingness (revealed in a lack of notice boards and publicity about activities), and changes brought about by social and geographical mobility.

This exploration reveals that belonging may well be stronger then believing as research participants confided their theological doubts but desired to remain 'chapel' because of identifying with this heritage (Bruce, 2010: 236). This study also points to a complex relationship between identity and religion: Bruce argues that the same conditions that can act to preserve a language can also preserve religious observance. However, he also notes that Nonconformist allegiance is losing its salience as a carrier of Welsh identity and that the Welsh Assembly Government and Welsh-medium schools also give Welsh people other avenues with which to assert their nationality. The increasingly bilingual nature of communities enables a more varied linguistic network of relating for people in early twenty-first-century Wales (Bruce, 2010: 236). Welsh people no longer need the chapels in order to evidence their Welshness, and, furthermore, they may well feel increasingly uncomfortable in a monolingual setting given the bilingual nature of the rest of their lives and relationships.

One difficulty in analysing and discussing religious trends in Wales is that they are changing fast. The main work looking at secularisation in Wales, Chambers's *Religion, Secularization and Social Change in Wales*, although published in 2005, is based on research undertaken at the end of the twentieth century. However I have been able to draw on the census and his later work, as well as Bruce's, research which seems at odds with public perception. There is a paucity of exploration and evidence regarding secularism in a Welsh context, and a need for more reflection and research.

It would be simplistic to regard Wales as merely a region within the UK, as there are significant differences between the different countries (and even regions) of the UK regarding religious history, practice and identity, and the relationship between them (Davie, 1994: 5). If Day (2011) is right that issues of national identity are key to understanding the socio-religious context in Britain, then this has a distinctive outworking within Wales, as it does within the other countries of the UK, although very little attention has been given to the analysis of secularism in Wales.

I have argued that the influence of Nonconformist Christianity within Wales is a *mythomoteur* rather than a description of any current reality, not least because of the distinct nature of secularism in Wales today. The historic roles of the different denominations in promoting and neglecting Welsh customs and artistic traditions is also more complex than the dominance of the myth of Nonconformist Wales would suggest. To call the Anglican Church *Yr Hen Estrones* (the stranger) is to ignore the vital role the Anglican Church has played at key stages in the history of Wales in preserving the language and customs, sometimes against a new resistance identity constructed by Nonconformist leaders. In the next chapter I explore why it was necessary to construct a new identity for Welsh people and, in particular, Welsh women.

4

Religion, Women and Wales

ANOTHER SALEM[14]

You walk in late, on your way
to your rightful place
at the margins, or ranked

silenced rows, where you will sit,
head bowed in feigned piety,
clutching your temple. So say

nothing when your accusers
see devils. Make yourself
small, curse the moment

you were ever centre-stage,
scrutinised, iconic,
selling your soul for soap. (Ceridwen, 2011a)

Images and stereotypes

Where are the women in the myths and images of Wales? Beddoe has identified a number of stereotypes and tropes within Welsh life but argues that 'Welsh women are culturally invisible', elaborating that 'Wales, land of my fathers, is a land of coalminers, rugby players and male voice choirs' (Beddoe, 1986: 227). Despite the industrialised and sporting macho stereotypes, there are also some key female tropes, most of which are aligned to religion and respectability. The 'Welsh Mam', an image reinforced in part by the film and television adaptations of the famous novel *How Green Was My Valley*, is an example of this, as 'the moral custodian of the home, keeping drink and trouble out' (Beddoe, 1986: 230).

Another cultural trope she notes is the Welsh Lady in Welsh costume. In 1834, Augusta Waddington Hall (Lady Llanover) won an essay competition in the Cardiff Royal Eisteddfod on the subject of the importance of speaking Welsh and preserving national costumes. Her original purpose was to reinvigorate the local economy by persuading women to wear indigenous tweed instead of cottons and calicoes, and although she did not describe the national costume in 1834, with the help of others she designed a costume based on peasant dresses and incorporating a cloak and tall beaver hat (Morgan, 1983: 80). It was quickly adopted in the media, in cartoons, postcards and pottery models as an archetypal image of Welsh women (Morgan, 1983: 80). Its popularity was reinforced into the next century by the prevalence of Vosper's painting *Salem* as one of the only pictures ordinary Welsh people were able to own as it was widely available with soap tokens as a homely, clean-living image.[15]

There is a tradition that the devil can be seen in the folds of the shawl because of the old lady's pride and that she is arriving late to chapel in order to make an impact with her new and elaborate outfit. My poem is, in part, a response to this (and with an allusion to the Salem witch trials) as well as a comment on the unfairness of making her centre stage only to criticise her for vanity. The reception of this famous image illustrates the unease with which a religious or pious woman is regarded. She is depicted on her way to her true place, in a pew as a consumer of ministry, a silent listener, rather than as someone who deserves recognition and a role in her own right. Furthermore, she is shamed in the traditions surrounding the picture.

According to Beddoe, the 'pious woman' is a characteristic Welsh image and she regards this as significant because 'the few women normally given mention in standard histories of Wales were models of piety' (Beddoe, 1986: 232); for example, Mary Jones of Bala who walked in bare feet for twenty-six miles in order to secure her own copy of the Bible, Madam Bevan who helped Griffith Jones with his circulating schools, the philanthropic Lady Charlotte Guest and the hymn writer Ann Griffiths.

There is also the counterpart to this image, that of the sexy Welsh woman, 'courting her partner in bed' and as I shall explore later, condemned by the Victorian Blue Books report for uncivilised wantonness (Beddoe, 1986: 234, 235). Beddoe's final image is of the funny woman. She refers to the Welsh characters in sitcoms such as Ruth Madoc's character in *Hi de Hi*, commenting that 'English people still regard Welsh people, along with Irish people, as inherently funny' and particularly women, as 'British Rail ticket collectors at Temple Meads or Paddington call you Blodwen' (Beddoe, 1986: 234, 236).

This brief discussion of images of Welsh women reinforces a view that religion, particularly Nonconformity, has influenced the identity of Welsh women. I will now further explore women and Nonconformity in a historical context.

Nonconformity and women

If there is general agreement that Nonconformity has influenced Welsh culture in the past, there is also similar agreement that this influence was particularly strong on women (Aaron and Rees, 1994: 11; Beddoe, 2000: 179; Peach, 2007: 166). An oral history project researching the lives of women from 1920–60, by Merched y Wawr (Hanes Merched Cymru 2002) revealed that almost every woman interviewed stated that church or chapel had played a fundamental role in their lives.

Although the participants were all within a certain age range, Welsh-speaking and from rural areas, it is still significant that such an overwhelming majority had such strong links with religious institutions. The participants in this project, despite condemning certain practices such as refusing communion to divorced women or unmarried mothers as callous, did not consider church or chapel as having 'oppressed' them. In fact they were highly critical of the suggestion. In emotive language the writers of the webpage of the project state:

> It is fashionable among some historians of Wales today, many of them the brightest of women in their fields in the tradition of the socialism of the industrial south, to ignore, ridicule or criticize the far-reaching influence of the chapel and dissent in Welsh history and especially when discussing women's history. It is claimed that this is a negative influence, which has hindered development, limited choice and oppressed women. But, on the basis of the research for this project, this has clearly not been the case. Whilst condemning the practice of the excommunication of innocent women, not one participant talked about being oppressed or restricted by the influence of the chapel on society.[16] (My translation)

The effect of religion on Welsh female identity, therefore, is controversial. My own reading of this comment is that religion has been such a key influence in the lives of women who are now elderly that criticism of it is upsetting and unwelcome. One participant, Marlis Jones,[17] describes how her aunt was refused communion because of her divorce (despite having experienced severe domestic violence) and would leave the chapel service immediately before communion was distributed in order to avoid the embarrassment of being rejected. The writers of the website maintain that these chauvinistic behaviours were roundly condemned by the research participants and attributed this to the fact that women did not hold positions of leadership or responsibility at the time. However, they did not consider themselves in any way repressed or oppressed by their church and chapel-going experience (Hanes Merched Cymru, 2002).

Others have argued that this influence has been detrimental to women. The artist Christine Kinsey, reflecting on her work, wrote:

> I have been asked again why I only paint women. Well, my answer is that it's the only thing I know anything about – being female, being Welsh and living and working in Wales whose culture has been dominated by Christianity. The continual horror stories about the treatment of women have been one of the reasons why the reassessment of the depiction and perception of women in society has been an integral part of my imagery and language. For many centuries in European Christian painting, women were mostly portrayed as virgins, martyrs and whores, as long-suffering victims without voice whose role was to enable and support others. These paintings were used to instruct people, who were unable to read, how man was created in God's image. (Kinsey, 2009: 33)

Her own work involves strong colours, particularly blue, and images of women which convey repression or silencing, as in one image from the collection *Colloquy* (the cover for this book) where one woman is naked and faceless and both women are in darkness,[18] a stark contrast to the woman represented in Vosper's *Salem* who is at the centre of the picture, in her bright shawl.

This is also a significant and pervasive theme within feminist writings in Wales. For example, Beddoe refers to Nonconformist chapels as historically 'the agency of the social control of women' (Beddoe, 2000: 177). Gramich and Brennan, in their comprehensive introduction to the anthology *Welsh Women's Poetry 1460–2001*, also refer to the still 'looming' effect of Nonconformity on Welsh culture (Gramich and Brennan, 2003: xviii). They comment that for people in Wales, chapel culture is associated with 'a barren asceticism, narrow-mindedness and sexual prudery' (Gramich and Brennan, 2003: xviii) and ascribe these characteristics as inherent not to Christianity in Wales, but to the deliberate attempts by Nonconformist leaders to create an identity for women based on chastity and morality. They argue that this was in response to a key event in recent Welsh history, one which Morgan refers to as a 'turning point', the publication and subsequent controversy of the *Reports of the Commissioners of Inquiry into the State of Education in Wales 1847*, the so-called Blue Books report (Morgan, 1983: 92).

Valleys and vaginas: the historical context

'Your lusts have found you out,' shouted Mr Parry and thump went his fist on the handrail, 'and you have paid the price of all women like you. Your body was the trap of the Devil and you allowed temptation to visit you. Now you bring an illegitimate child into the world against the commandment of God. Thou shalt not commit adultery. Prayer is wasted on your sort and you are not fit to enter the House of God. You shall be cast forth into the outer darkness until you have learned your lesson.' (Llewellyn, 2001: 104, 105)

The fictional account of the casting out of a pregnant woman in the novel (and later film) *How Green Was My Valley* (Llewellyn, 2001) is an iconic image of Welsh chapel culture: Aaron argues that the dominant male virtuous deacon 'hounding out' a sexually permissive woman is 'a characteristically Welsh image' (Aaron, 1994: 184). In the book, the narrator, a little boy, responds angrily to the hypocrisy of the chapel minister and elders, angering his mother but gaining the respect of his father. However, this scene has perpetuated the representation of Welsh Nonconformity as repressive, cruel and even misogynistic.

Although it was a common experience, it was not universal; for example, one participant in the Merched y Wawr oral history project describes how she was not cast out of chapel when she fell pregnant out of wedlock, but sensed that she should stop attending for a while and come back when her daughter had been born, for her baptism:

We weren't turned out of chapel. No one would have told me not to go, but I felt that this is what I should do ... it was my choice, no one stopped me ... it was my choice to go back as a member – I was still a member.[19] (My translation)

The previous exploration of the historical context of discussions about Welsh identity has revealed a complex picture of the influence of religious movements on Welsh culture as well as ambivalence as to the role of the dominant Christian traditions in both strengthening and diminishing Welsh customs and artistic pursuits. An important element in these discussions has been controversies about the appropriateness and respectability of different activities, as seen in Welsh attitudes towards alcohol and sexual activity in the last two hundred years.

However, a religiously repressive attitude towards sexuality is a relatively recent phenomenon as Welsh women's poetry shows. This body of work, originating from the fifteenth century, records the coexistence of erotic and devotional themes often in the same poem, which Gramich and Brennan call the 'bi-textuality' of the Welsh tradition (Gramich and Brennan, 2003: xvii). The best example of this is in the work of one of the earliest poets, Gwerful Mechain (1460–1502) who wrote *An Ode to the Vagina* and several similar poems. In her praise poem to the vagina she exclaims:

Trwsglwyn merch, drud annerch dro, / Berth addwyn, Duw'n borth iddo.

[A girl's thick glade, it is full of love / Lovely bush, blessed be it by God above.]
(Gramich and Brennan, 2003: 2, 3)

The prevalence of bodily and erotic themes in Gwerful Mechain's religious poetry is shocking and is unrecognisable to us today as an acceptable expression of Welsh womanhood. What happened in the intervening years between a religious praise poem to the vagina and the shaming of the pregnant unmarried woman in *How Green Was My Valley?* The answer lies in the furore surrounding the publication of the *Reports of the Commissioners of Inquiry into the State of Education in Wales 1847* (the so-called Blue Books). In the response to the report it could be argued that a new resistance identity emerged for women, one that was deliberately and carefully constructed and is influential even today.

Blue Books and green valleys

Although the initial request for a report on the state of learning in Wales came from a Welshman, William Williams, ostensibly to encourage the improvement of education, it is also possible that there were concerns held by Williams and others about the 'uncivilised' nature of Welsh people given the prevalence of their political and religious dissent (Aaron, 1994: 185). Certainly the methodology and findings of the report were not restricted to educational matters as much of what was written was a thinly disguised attack on the sexual morals of Welsh women.

For example, the vicar of Nefyn (my own home town) was highly critical of his female parishioners' morality compared to that of English women and commented that 'in England farmers' daughters are respectable; in Wales they are in the constant habit of being courted in bed' and complained that he had to lock the bedroom windows of his female servants to stop them from letting men in at night.[20] This immorality was 'proof' that Wales needed to be civilised, or rather Anglicised – instilled with the values and language of the English middle classes (Aaron, 1994: 185, 186). This gave political leaders moral authority to attempt to eradicate the Welsh language and culture (Aaron, 1994: 186).

Anglican clergy used this inquiry for their own ends in order to condemn the rapidly growing Free Churches and sow seeds of doubt regarding the morality of the new churches (Aaron, 1994: 186); the 'evidence' for the licentious and barbaric behaviour of Welsh people, particularly the women, largely came from their own biased reporting (Morgan, 1983: 93).

The result was increased antagonism between Anglicanism and the Free Churches, to swell nationalistic feeling and for Nonconformist Welsh leaders themselves to display a 'hard-headed' and shrewd response in order to safeguard the reputation of their new and growing movement (Morgan, 1983: 93).

This resulted in the policing of the sexual behaviour of women in order to safeguard the reputation of the Free Churches (Aaron, 1994: 187) and the promotion of a respectable and genteel womanhood. One strategy was to publish a women's magazine called *Y Gymraes*, edited initially by Ieuan Gwynedd, a prominent minister and defender of the morality of Welsh women. The dilemma posed for the generation of women who were grandmothers and mothers to Welsh women living today is well illustrated by Aaron:

> The late nineteenth-century Welsh woman seems, then, to have been presented with three possibilities in terms of choosing an identity. Either she abandoned her Welsh allegiances and adopted the English middle-class model of refined femininity, however inappropriate it may have been to her cultural roots and her social position; or she defensively asserted her Welshness in the face of insult and, to prove its virtues, clad herself in an armour of strict propriety which would inevitably have entailed self-suppression on a larger scale than mere self-control; or she accepted the English definition of herself as the libidinous hoyden of primitive Wild Wales. None of these possible identities afforded her a voice of her own. (Aaron, 1994: 188)

Aaron's comments illustrate the argument that a new Welsh female identity was created for women using a particular repressive and respectable form of Nonconformity, in order to save the reputation of Welsh people as a whole. There was some critique and protest at the findings of the 1847 report, for example Robert Jones Derfel wrote a satirical play published in 1854 entitling it *Brad y Llyfrau Gleision* (The Treachery of the Blue Books). However Saunders Lewis, in his lecture 'Tynged yr Iaith',[21] which is credited as bringing about the birth of the Welsh Language Society and nationalist movement, referred to this report several times and was highly critical that Welsh people, despite initial anger and upset, had accepted and even submissively implemented the recommendations. Brooks argues that the response to the report shows that greater offence had been taken to the claim of immorality than to the need for Welsh people to learn English, and that the importance assigned to the creation of a moral identity, rather than safeguarding the language, was one of the factors in the demise of Welsh as a national language (Brooks, 2015: 76–9).

Cleanliness is next to godliness: The Welsh Mam

> … You are king in the chapel. But I will be queen in my own kitchen![22]

> (Angharad to Mr Gruffydd, the Minister, in the film version of *How Green Was My Valley*.)

A new emphasis on morality was only one part of this constructed identity for Welsh women. Another important instrument was the stereotype of the Welsh Mam and the location of Welsh women in the home (Pilcher, 1994: 31). Beddoe (1989) demonstrates that at different times during the past century the ideology of the woman as wife and mother has been deliberately constructed in response to social pressures, such as the need for women to 'go back to home and duty' in order to free up roles and jobs for men returning from the Second World War. Pilcher's (1994) research with different cohorts of women demonstrates that successive younger generations revealed more egalitarian attitudes towards housework between men and women and a lessening of what she calls an 'invest-ment' of their feminine identities in the domestic sphere although they still, at that time, did the bulk of the work, despite their egalitarian beliefs and paid work commitments (Pilcher, 1994: 45).

Even if women were responsible for the work, the stereotype of the Welsh Mam also meant that some of the power was held by the woman. For example 'Eirlys', a research participant in a study by Brown and Baker, comments that her mother was 'boss in the house' (Brown and Baker, 2011: 63) and although the domestic sphere could be limiting, the influence of these mothers and other female role models could be significant, 'far greater than most accounts of history in Wales have accounted for' (Brown and Baker, 2011: 81).

Mannay (2016), however, argues that the ideology of the Welsh Mam is still current, and exerts pressure on Welsh women not just to work harder within the home, but to also feel shame and stigmatisation when they cannot reach their own high standards of juggling paid work with keeping a clean and tidy house. Mannay's research participants invested their own moral identities in their roles as mothers and wives (Mannay, 2016: 74), seeing cleanliness as an important aspect of performing (working-class) respectability (75).

Arguably, there is more pressure on women who are working class 'when the metaphorical stereotypes of your class are muck, filth, dirt and waste products' (75), and Mannay attributes this pressure Welsh women feel as a continuing response to the Blue Books report (75). Women continue to do the bulk of the housework because it lessens the guilt they feel about being selfish in having paid work or inadequacy at their performance of motherhood (79, 82). There is no wonder therefore that Lord Leverhulme bought *Salem* as a wholesome image of Welsh womanhood, giving prints away with packets of Lever soap and seeing it as entirely within character for the central figure in her new shawl to be vilified and shamed for her 'pride'.

In this discussion of the stereotypes of women in Wales, we have seen the important role that religion has played in creating a repressed and respectable image, in response to the politically motivated criticisms of the women of Wales in the Blue Books report. The assertion that Nonconformist Christianity has oppressed women is, however, controversial – not least amongst older women who have found their identity in their memories of childhood involvement in church and chapel and the importance of religion in their own life stories. The Welsh Mam and the woman in Welsh costume immortalised in the *Salem* image are two significant examples of stereotypes whose influence remains today. However these tropes are complex in that they both value women's significance and limit them: the Welsh Mam's power is at the expense of drudgery and hard work, and the woman in the Welsh costume in *Salem* is vilified for her pride. At this significant period in Wales's relationship with religion, the next stage of this research is to find out what kind of identity Welsh women currently enact, through hearing about their experiences. How do they describe their identities through their life stories? How has religion impacted on their lives?

5

Life Stories

Introduction

I conducted thirteen narrative interviews during 2011–12, which also included some discussion around stereotypes and images of Welsh women. Amongst my sample, two women identified as either atheist or agnostic (Jinny and Jessie), three as occasional but not regular church or chapel-goers (Stefania, Hannah and Helen), three with a current Church in Wales affiliation (Lucy, Harriet and Elinor), three with a current Free Church affiliation (Marged, Sera and Bethan) and two with a strong Christian affiliation but non-denominational (Yvette and Stacey). Yvette later became an Anglican and Bethan had been brought up as a Roman Catholic. Stefania regarded herself to have been brought up as a Catholic, though she had also made her own decision as an older child to be confirmed in the Anglican Church in order to fit in with the other children.

All the women considered themselves to be wholly or partly Welsh. All had been born in Wales apart from Yvette who had been born in America to parents from a Welsh heritage and Harriet who had been born in England. Stefania, although born in Wales, had an Italian father and regarded herself as dual heritage Italian–Welsh.

I analysed the narratives as wholes, using a reflective approach informed by discourse analysis, and looked at common themes in more detail. I coded sentences according to the themes which I had already identified, as well as those which arose naturally from the initial analysis. I also reflected on the interview experience as well as the transcripts as wholes before breaking them up thematically, and I have gained insight into the experience of the women both from complete narratives and the comparison of themes and how the different stories of the women interact with one another.

I have decided to present one account as a case study in order to explore the way the themes often intertwine within a life story. Then I shall discuss the dominant themes within all of the research conversations. All the names are pseudonyms and I have anonymised any details which could identify any of the participants.

Elinor: a case study

Some of my participants' life stories were particularly coherent and dramatic. This was true of Elinor and her story is an example of how religion has played a formative influence on her life, not just in terms of faith but also within the Welsh discourses of repression and respectability.

Elinor was born in (as she termed it) an 'unmarried mothers' home' after her mother fell pregnant. She was brought up by her grandmother whom she thought of as her own mother until she was ten years old. These were scandalous circumstances at the time. She said:

> When I was born in the 1960s life wasn't as it is today – women couldn't have children outside marriage, well they could but it was scorned upon. My birth father was the son of our minister in our chapel and at that time, in those days, scandals within the Church were tried to be forgotten about. My father at the time, my grandfather or adopted father if you want to call him, he was also the Church secretary, so my whole life has been involved around the chapel then that I was brought up in.

She characterised her background as Welsh middle-class and chapel-orientated; her father was in a professional and high-status role within the community. However, she had had a variety of religious experiences growing up and because of the different influences of family and friends had experienced both Catholic and evangelical groups and worship.

The shock of finding out about her real parentage and losing her grandfather (whom she had thought of as her father) when she was a teenager led her to question her faith. She also struggled with the normal pressures of growing up: boys and drinking, both of which clashed with her evangelical faith. This led her to feel guilty and have low self-esteem:

> I know he [Jesus] died for me and I believed in that … but you do go along with the flow and what I found then was that as I was into my teens and you do things like drinking and meeting boys and those sort of things you felt quite bad about it and felt sinful about it and I found that I was very … very, well between everything I started self-harming and doing different things, because I felt worthless.

Later on, Elinor's experience of church as a young wife and mother was that there was a lot of hypocrisy and a clash between the conservative and liberal values (for example on appropriate clothing for church) of the different generations. This resulted in her turning her back on institutional religion. At around this time she gradually realised that she and her husband were growing apart and she also made contact with a birth sister. Her birth mother had already had another child by the same father, who had been given up for adoption and was therefore a full sibling. This child took steps to find her real family and for Elinor, getting to know her (Pauline) was a turning point:

> It was quite strange, it was as if somebody had plugged a hole for me when she came back, because I suppose all through my formative years there was something missing. We weren't twins or anything, but I just felt as if there was something missing. It could have been God maybe and that I wasn't searching deep enough or whatever, but when

Pauline came back then and she was a vicar and her husband was a vicar and it just made me realise that we are all human and we are all frail and fragile in different ways.

Pauline's faith and role as an ordained person and commitment as a Christian led Elinor to find her own faith again and, ironically, to leave her husband and embrace a fully embodied and human Christian faith, one that accepted mistakes and aspects of life which had been frowned upon in her upbringing, for example alcohol:

[Her relationship with Pauline] made me realise that you could go for a drink and you could have a glass of wine, even though I did that, but growing up in the sort of family that I did before – you were going to hell, you know. It is quite strange really. But even though I knew that wasn't so, I think it follows the way you think and you think you're not good enough, or you have to be pious or whatever. But by meeting Pauline and Andrew, it was a case of ... I could be me. I could be me and follow Christ and be a Christian and be fragile and everything and be human really.

And, somewhere the strength came for me to leave my husband. So I told my mother then, you know. 'Well, what's taken you so long to do it?', or something like that she said. 'I've been so many years now too frightened to tell you in case I upset you, you know' and this was it.

This part of the interview revealed many interesting aspects to the ambivalent effect of religion and faith on Elinor. It gave her a confidence to make her own decisions, whilst also restricting her and inducing in her a sense of anxiety about what others (especially her adopted mother – birth grandmother) would think. Her faith had been an ambivalent influence on her life: she had reported earlier how her guilt stemming from her sense of failure at being a Christian had also led to her self-harming. Her faith had also been a great source of strength and comfort to her. Yet religion had contributed culturally to the pressures that Elinor and her family felt to be 'respectable' and the sense of shame they felt when Elinor's birth mother had fallen pregnant:

It was all secrets and dynamics going on around our family life really, you know. Being that time my birth mother, my sister, was made to feel unclean and dirty and she had lots of issues due to that and I think in those days that was what people did – you went to chapel and you had to be like this and had to be like that. 'What would Mrs Jones think and what would Mrs So and So down the road ...?' and I think that has made me completely reverse, because I don't care what people think.

People can take me as I am and if they don't like that I'm Elinor, this is me and I can only give you me and I think that taught me a lot growing up. Also seeing the way people judged each other, I try my best not to be judgemental, even though we are because we are human. But I've taught my sons that as well, not to look down at anybody else.

This sense of shame and thinking through the effect on her family led Elinor, ironically, to a growing confidence and agency. Yet, it seemed from Elinor's comments that her (grand)mother had been restricted by her own religion and the pressures of community life:

When I look at photos of her when she was away nursing, she went to Llandudno and she nursed lords and ladies and there are photos of her on holidays and we laugh about this now and there she was with bottles of Newky Brown around her lying on a beach with her friends and there's a gang of boys there.

Yet, I am wondering whether she didn't want to come home, because she had the freedom in England to do what she wanted to; she wouldn't have been able to do that in a small Welsh community. And yet, these photos ... because she was a nurse she said she smoked because of all the cancer patients she had and the stench and that was the only way. Yet when I used to smoke and I used to drink; it was taboo. So there were two extremes of thought there.

She regarded her (grand)mother as someone who had instilled feminism in her. She also admired her caring nature and her strength.

When I asked Elinor about stereotypes of Welsh women she also referred to the woman as being strong and considered that chapel was more 'Welsh' and that the different denominations had different stereotypes:

I think there is a stereotype of Welsh women, I think women who go to chapel. I grew up in a small village near Neath and there was a congregational chapel there, there was a Baptist chapel there, up the road in the next village the Methodist ... you know you have the whole lot, Catholic, everything ... But you found that perhaps the women who went to chapel were more matronly you know, more ... I know this sounds awful because women ... curtains, looking at people and saying you shouldn't do this you shouldn't do that ... and not looking at themselves whereas I found maybe people going to churches didn't seem so ... they were more laid back maybe.

Whereas again in Catholic churches you have the idea of the Catholic club and they meet together and they have a drink whereas in Nonconformity sometimes alcohol is taboo. I remember my grandmother telling me I wasn't allowed to play cards because they were things of the devil, you know! I don't know, so I think we do stereotype. I have a stereotype of chapel women in my head ... Chapel is more Welshness as well. I think of chapel I think of Welshness and Welsh ... the Church is more Anglicised ... I don't know ... women seem more genteel.

Elinor's story demonstrates some of the features of the historical and sociological research in previous chapters: denominations are described on a sliding scale of 'Welshness' and chapel culture seen as more restrictive in terms of alcohol and sexuality. This was regulated not by the leadership but by other members of the community, what Elinor refers to as 'what would Mrs Jones down the road think'. For Elinor, these women seemed to gain a sense of self-esteem from being respectable, however for Elinor herself her self-esteem and confidence came from a clear sense of her own identity and agency and not caring about the mythical Mrs Jones and her opinions.

Elinor describes a personal faith which led her to divorce her husband and gave her the confidence to make the right decision for her; this tolerant Christianity, one which has experienced several denominations and influences and which embraces difference gave her the resources to face the messiness of life.

Her story exemplified many of the themes and attitudes of my other participants, as well as demonstrating the difference between the generations. There was a significant difference between how Elinor and her (grand)mother viewed respectability and its effect on their agency – in fact Elinor's identity could be said to have been formed in reaction against this repressive 'chapel' culture. This was also an important theme for my other participants.

Repression and respectability

The discourse of repression and negative attitudes to the body, sexuality and drinking was a major aspect of the religion that had formed the cultural backdrop to the early lives of most of my participants. None felt that these prohibitions and traditional teachings should remain in place. They were aware of the shame involved with transgressing these norms and the pressure to be respectable had been a negative influence on their lives. If they were mothers, this had not been something they had wanted to pass on to their own children.

Comparing the restrictiveness of the different denominations and their attitudes to sex and drink was a common theme. Most regarded this as part of 'chapel' rather than 'church' culture. Sera for example used the word *sychdduwiol* (literally 'dry-godly') to refer to her image of repressed Welsh chapel-goers, miserable in attitude as well as teetotal. She contrasted her own experience of chapel now, where the congregation can be 'themselves', to a hypocrisy and a negativity which still haunts those in older generations. She ascribed this restrictive and shaming Christianity as the reason why many men did not attend chapel anymore and recounted the experience of her father:

> I just go back to my father, he doesn't go regularly now, even though he was brought up as a three times on a Sunday kind of a man, he just remembers the sermons which ranted against the different elements of society and my dad liked a pint every so often but he was made to feel … well as though he wanted to disappear under the seat. He still can't get over that to an extent. The feeling of not being good enough to come along, even though he is very supportive, proud of Mam for being an elder …

A story she told to illustrate this further was of a group clearing the vestry before selling it along with the chapel house. They came across anti-drink pledge cards signed by people they knew who drank alcohol, which they found very amusing.

Jessie felt she had 'more to say' to the Anglican Church (although she was an agnostic) because of its less repressive image. She found the dominant Calvinistic Methodism of Wales oppressive. She acknowledged how this culture had 'kept the language alive' but had 'killed the dancing' and felt that it is 'one of the narrowest religions'. She further linked this conservative, repressive Calvinistic Methodism with Plaid Cymru and the Welsh middle class, often using all three labels in the same phrase. She had severe criticism for this section of Welsh society, bolstered by a hypocritical religion, a 'monster' that had been created to dominate others.

Harriet hardly spoke about the Free Churches and their influence, instead describing a Christianity which was attractive and earthy. When I asked her about this she condemned what she saw as a Free Church influence in the strongest of terms and its effect on others:

> I do know people who have been quite brutalised by their chapel culture. So, there was one young man who came to a group I ran in prison. It was an English prison but he was from Wales, lived all of his life in Wales. I remember the other chaplain saying to this man whom I will call 'John' (not his name): 'John, you always paint everything as black. It's not black in a chapel.' And he [John] said, 'if you came to my chapel you would know it was black, it is only ever black. It's black on every day of the week. It's black. And I will never go back inside a chapel building.'

For Bethan, however, her Catholic upbringing had been stricter than anything she had experienced within her local chapel. It was:

> ... Not strict in that we had to sit down and read the Bible. It wasn't like that at all! But just ...what my Mam had drummed in to me for example since I was twelve 'you can't come home pregnant ... We would kick you out.' I knew they would never do that and that kind of thing. I would be scared even to consider ... I wasn't that kind of a child anyway but ... when I was going out, when I was sixteen I knew I wouldn't drink because I knew I wouldn't be able to go out again ... my parents were terrified I would get drunk and sleep with someone.

The sense that 'chapel' was currently repressive was not borne out in Sera's story either and she described several instances where she received exceptional support both from her family and her Nonconformist church. As a young single woman she became pregnant after a brief relationship and had a child. The fact that the minister at the time supported her unreservedly she considers to be one of the main factors which helped her on her Christian journey. Although she did not say this at the time of the interview, she texted me later in the day to say:

> One thing I forgot to say which was important in terms of my own faith journey. The minister insisted that we had a baptism in the chapel and not at home so that she [the baby] wasn't any different from anyone else. This was a key moment in getting people on our side. I understand that he even preached a sermon which helped turn some who were against us, to be supportive of us. If he hadn't done all that I am sure I would have been turned off religion for life.

Her story was more confessional than the other interviews and as well as telling me about her faith journey, she also told me about the process of coming out as a gay woman (though she is not fully 'out' in the sense that only some family members and some colleagues and friends know she is a lesbian). However, both her chapel-elder mother and her minister are highly supportive of her and her sexuality. In fact, her denomination is ambivalent rather than negative towards homosexuality, seeing it as an English phenomenon:

> The impression you get from [the denominational newspaper] is that we are talking about an 'us and them'. It's OK for these gay people, probably English people, living in a city, it's OK for them to have their civil partnerships but they need to leave us alone and not come to our chapels. Why would they want to come?

Given her story and experience of not being able to be fully honest about herself, I would have expected Sera to have felt more alienated and unhappy with the church, but in her interview she gave the impression of someone who was rooted in her community, supported by a strong mother (whom she called her hero). She was frustrated by the hypocrisy of chapel culture which she noticed in other chapels, but not her own. She considered her own chapel as a place where she could be 'herself' to a certain extent. Her minister knows she is gay and supports her.

My participants described a Wales which is changing and even a chapel culture that is ambivalent or even supportive in practice of a more accepting attitude towards different forms of sexuality and alcohol. Although the repressive respectability of the past has influenced the backgrounds of the women in this study, these findings suggest that this effect will gradually diminish as families fail to socialise their children into the fear of 'what Mrs Jones down the road' will say, as Elinor's story exemplified.

Faith and the Church

Individual faith versus institutional religion

A theme that was important for many of my research participants was distinguishing between individual faith and institutional religion. Yvette spoke about a sense of decay in the traditional denominations and Stacey, Stefania, Jinny, Helen and Jessie used the word 'boring' to describe some of their early experiences of church or chapel. Both Harriet and Lucy had had highly negative experiences working for the church or Christian organisations.

A major criticism by most of the participants was the hypocrisy of those involved in church. For this generation, churchgoing is seen as the pursuit of an older generation. Yvette said:

> My husband has preached in several churches and I have come along too … they weren't so thriving and you could feel the damp on the walls and smell the must and you knew the age demographic of the church, if they didn't have some new people coming in the church it wasn't going to last.

Bethan was the only interviewee to say that she had 'enjoyed' going to church as a young person and the only one not to have a discourse of boredom when speaking about institutional religion (though Hannah also said that when she had gone to church in her early married life she had enjoyed it as it 'lifted her out' of her life).

The positive aspects of religion were mainly to do with individual faith and for some, to a lesser extent, the support of a local congregation. Sera gained great strength from Psalm 27, which had helped her come to terms with her sexuality, and her faith and support from her minister at the time had helped her and her family cope with her mother's serious illness. For Yvette and Sera there was also a sense of belonging in church, Yvette speaking about church as family for her, especially as she lived so far away from her own American home.

Individual faith had helped several of my participants to grow and flourish. Traditional church teaching may have seemed at odds with this: for Sera, God had helped her accept being gay and for Elinor, her relationship with the divine gave her the strength to divorce her husband. For these women, an experience of God and the teaching of institutional religion were often contradictory.

For Lucy, religion was more of an internal and personal experience; her unjust treatment within a Christian institution had not affected her faith, which she considered to be a factor in her high level of confidence and self-esteem. Similarly, Sera, despite oppressive Christian attitudes towards homosexuality, ascribed her security and confidence to her faith, which has 'kept her going' and 'supported' her.

The only person to critique the institution directly was Harriet, who regarded churches as seeking to control and dominate rather than enable flourishing. She was particularly critical here of the Anglican Church, its rules about ministry and how services had to be according to prescribed rites:

> I now question what parts of the ritual are bridges to open spirituality and helping people come in a relationship with Christ and what are the rituals that bring people into a submissive relationship with the organisation of the church. I think there is a difference … I now find myself questioning more and more whether the churches and organised religion are focusing on the love of Christ and spirit of Christ or the practices that keep themselves in a position of power and authority over people.

Harriet spoke about God using female rather than male metaphors and felt that as an ordained minister now no longer paid by the church, she could reach out to people more effectively with a similar spirituality. This relationship with God was more Celtic, even pre-Christian:

> Now, in a way I see that [spirituality] as more connected in many ways to a pre-Christian Celtic richness that is here in Wales as it is in other Celtic countries … I think there is a Celtic tradition where that is more visceral. It's more something which you can sense, it's a sensual presence in areas where there is a tradition of pre-Celtic tradition, almost a pagan tradition. I mean don't want to sound a bit new age-ish but there is a tradition of prayer before the name of God was known through Christ.

Harriet wanted to make a distinction between religion and spirituality from the start of the conversation. She regarded God as 'an experience of something that connects everything, connects me within the universe and something outside myself', and this experience of connectedness had been with her before she even identified as a Christian. She was critical of the rules and regulations of the (Anglican) Church, which she regarded as a means of control and of excluding people. Her experience of the inappropriate behaviour directed towards her when she was an ordained minister was compounded by the inaction of church authorities and a failure to take the behaviour seriously. She struggled with finding her identity outside this all-encompassing role of ministry, but she felt she had no choice but to remain outside the official ministry of the church. She felt that in a secular role she could be a better bridge between God and ordinary people. Because of her experience, she had felt voiceless, but now she felt better able to speak on behalf of those who are disempowered by the church.

Her story also showed the importance of the role of religious institutions in helping or frustrating the flourishing of those who work within them. Harriet's and, to some extent, Lucy's stories revealed what can happen when individuals and groups misuse their positions and power, and the resulting emotional harm when people behave badly within Christian organisations and churches. And yet their experience and the experiences of others in my sample who were Christians was that their personal faith, despite the institutions, was resilient.

Pastoral care and local church experience

The importance of good pastoral care and a positive local church experience was something that arose unexpectedly in several interviews. The practice of pastoral care on a local level had had a significant impact on the women's lives. I have already mentioned the difficult and even emotionally abusive experiences within church life and other Christian institutions that some of my participants had experienced. Hypocrisy, along with misogyny and sexism, often made the church a deeply unattractive place for many of the women. There were several stories of churches not practising what they preached, including Jessie's recollection of her own experience of attending her local chapel as a child where the two organists in a small congregation had a disagreement and had not spoken for decades.

Good experiences of pastoral care highlighted by my participants included a minister father encouraging his daughter to try out new and varied experiences and supporting her in this, church communities which provided a non-judgemental, accepting home for some of my participants in a low-key way and the support of a minister who had shown compassion and empathy to a family by sharing her own experience of a debilitating illness. This good practice could be characterised as supportive, encouraging and 'unprofessional' in so far as ministers shared their own experiences (for example of illness) rather than keeping a professional and boundaried distance. An unobtrusive, supportive approach had made a significant difference in the lives of some of the women and had contributed to their growth and flourishing.

However, both Stacey and Marged described astonishing levels of sexism in their own church experiences. For Stacey, this meant leaving one particular church, part of a worldwide evangelical denomination, because of its misogyny.

> It's not maybe an issue as much for the church we're in now, but in the past and the last church we were in the leader was very sexist and he would say from the front, in one church service he was on about this minibus which goes around town picking up all the women to go to a nightclub and it says on the minibus 'no fat ugly chicks allowed'. And he said from the front of the pulpit, I want this church to be like the minibus which goes around town, I don't want any fat ugly chicks in this church – from the front, in a sermon!

Stacey was very critical of this. In her work as a mental health professional she was aware that this could have been painful for some women in the congregation who might have experienced sexual and emotional abuse; she also described other instances where the female members were pressurised to be physically attractive as they were the 'Bride of Christ'.

She further explained that the preacher made many jokes at the expense of his mother from the pulpit and although Stacey regarded this teaching as not being characteristically Welsh, perhaps the critique of his mother was. The preacher's mother conformed in many ways to the Welsh Mam stereotype and therefore this was one way of 'getting back' at her in Stacey's view. The church's men's club promoted this view of wives (and mothers) as people who needed to be controlled, or people who were annoying in some way:

> But that attitude of that church leader was because his mother was so dominating, very Welsh dominating mother, the matriarch if you like and I think he over the years had a very negative view of women. And it's because of his upbringing I think. He was very controlled so it's his way of rebelling now, he's in his late forties but any opportunity … like you see on their website they've got a men's night that they have once a month and they were putting down about, I can't remember what part of the Bible it's from (you probably remember) but something like one man can speak one word of sense but hundreds of words of nonsense come out of a woman's mouth, something like that, there's nothing worse than a nagging wife, like a dripping tap.

Stacey described a church culture which disparaged women whilst claiming to respect them and value their difference from men. The leader wielded power over the church, claiming that to go against his teaching or decisions was to go against God himself, using the language of 'theocracy' in order to bolster his own position. However, Stacey was critical of his lack of accountability. Her response was simply to leave and attend another evangelical church which has a less shaming attitude towards women, where power is shared amongst the leadership and people.

Marged also shared stories which revealed a lack of respect towards women. One story was about a male minister's disparaging attitude towards a young woman's contribution to a Bible class, as well as Marged's own encouragement of her:

> I was attending a Bible study arranged by someone else with a group of youngsters, mainly girls, who didn't go to chapel much, or study the Bible much. We were looking at a portion of scripture and no one was saying very much at all. I was so shocked because one girl piped up 'oh, yes I think this says so and so', I can't remember what it was now, and I said 'Well done, for saying this.' The leader, a Presbyterian minister said 'No, you're wrong.'

> MANON: Really?

> MARGED: Yes. 'You're wrong.' And I was so angry. I didn't feel confident enough then but now I would say 'do you mind!' because it had taken a lot for her to say what she had said and for them to say 'you're wrong. This is what it says and this is what it means' was unacceptable.

> So I haven't really taken my group to that minister again … [He also said] If you don't have a boy or girlfriend God will make sure you get one. So one of my boys in the youth group said, 'well can he make sure that my girlfriend doesn't have spots or spectacles?!' And I was thinking, 'oh great', I just wanted to leave. It's a responsibility for youth leaders working with young people, young women especially but also boys …

Although Marged and Stacey's experiences had not alienated them as Christians, it is alarming that recent church experience for middle-aged women reveals cultures of shaming and belittling women and girls and their contribution. If good pastoral care can help the flourishing of women, then negative experiences can be emotionally and spiritually damaging and, ultimately, can deter women from involvement in church life.

Denominationalism

A majority of the participants had some kind of a church or chapel background, though Harriet was not brought up as a Christian and made her own decision to be baptised as an adult. Several had switched denominations in the course of their lives and the women saw denominations as irrelevant.

Mari and Marged had remained in their own Free Church denomination and Lucy had remained an Anglican. However Elinor had moved from Congregationalism to Anglicanism, Bethan had changed from Roman Catholicism to Presbyterianism and Hannah had changed allegiance from Mormonism to the Church in Wales. Although Lucy expressed an admiration of the pioneer spirit within the Church in Wales and Marged was positive about the egalitarian nature of Congregationalism, there was no sense in which any of the Christian participants were wedded to their denomination or considered it to be a superior expression of Christianity; this exclusivity was seen as belonging to the generation of their parents. Although Marged was very positive about her Congregationalism, she was also keen to experiment and grow in her Christian experience when she was at college:

> I decided to study music and when I went to college they [Marged's parents] assumed I would attend the local Congregational chapel but I thought no, actually. Maybe they are a bit old fashioned! What I did was go to the Baptist church, near my halls, as they had a crowd of young people and then I found myself in the Anglican chaplaincy. Their service was later than the others! I went to another Baptist church but by my second year I had found a crowd in the chaplaincy and I liked the order of service and the chaplain, I enjoyed being there and we had the opportunity to go to Iona, Taizé and had a Taizé service in the chaplaincy every week, so I've had lots of different Christian experiences growing up.

The way in which denominationalism was seen as important for her parents' generation but not her own was clear in Bethan's interview and in her difficulty in making her own decision to break away from her Catholic background and attend a Presbyterian church. Issues of personal identity were tied up with denominational identity for her and she was afraid of upsetting her parents. Her decision had been largely based on wanting to embrace a more Welsh way of life for herself and her family. She could not make up her mind in the interview as to whether she regarded herself as a Catholic or a Presbyterian and settled on the term 'Christian' if she had to choose. Deciding to baptise her children in a chapel rather than the Catholic Church had been painful for her.

The lack of importance ascribed to denominations by my research participants was significant and they described this as something that was different from previous generations. This is clearly one feature of the changes in the practice of religion in Wales today.

Agency, self-esteem and confidence

I was interested to find out what the women thought and felt about their own identity. Several of my participants were tentative in interview (for example Bethan), unused to speaking about themselves (Stacey) and were concerned at the end of the interview as to whether they had spoken too much or been boring (Hannah and Harriet). The most interesting response to the question about telling me their life story was Jinny's, who gave me a one-sentence answer: 'Well, there isn't much of a story to my life. I was born. I went to school, college, went back home and then I went to work and that's it really.' However, Jinny also made the strongest statement of all the interviewees about agency. In discussing famous Welsh women she said: 'Nothing can stop anyone from doing what they want if they have the talent … Women can get ahead if they have the *nous* to do what they want to do.'

Bethan gave the clearest example of what it was like to struggle with feelings of low self-esteem and this was linked to her being bullied growing up as a Catholic, when other girls at school would make gun gestures at her, mouthing that she was a member of the IRA:

> I have always had low self-esteem and feel ugh! (hollow laugh) very often and it doesn't take a lot for someone to say something small and I turn it into something big and negative … Paranoia is the main thing that I have, what people think [of me] because some girls have been nasty, saying things over different periods of my life but that has nothing to do with religion, though sometimes it has come into it like this IRA business … (gesture of a gun with her fingers) shooting me down …

Bethan spoke about a sense of silencing, that being scared of family and friends' disapproval meant that she had become very shy, choosing not to say anything rather than being told off for what she might say.

I was surprised at the level of confidence and agency amongst the participants, given that I had been prompted to study this subject because the women I knew in my personal life and through work had seemed under-confident. In my initial coding of the responses I found an ambivalence. Often, sentences that I had coded as having a negative self-image were immediately followed by a sentence demonstrating a positive self-image and vice versa. For these women a positive and negative sense of self was often held in tension, and difficult experiences were utilised for personal growth.

Bethan for example saw her shyness (what I have termed a 'silencing') as positive because it stopped her from gabbling when she spoke and to be careful of what she said. Elinor's difficult personal experiences had helped her to grow and flourish and help others. Hannah also described a process of growing in confidence, of empathising with others and being a generally stronger person as an adult despite the experience of divorce and growing up with an alcoholic mother.

Harriet felt that her experiences had helped her speak on behalf of the voiceless and, like Elinor, that her experiences would help others. Lucy and Marged expressed a sense of confidence stemming from faith itself. Any empowerment that the women felt that arose from religion, as I have reported, came from the women's own faith and relationship with God and not generally from their experience of the institutional church.

For example, Marged's interview revealed positive self-esteem arising from faith: '… for me the gospel makes you confident. It makes you happy in who you are. God has created me … like this. Definitely.' She exhibited a strong sense of agency and recounted stories where she had stood up for the rights of women in chapel life:

> I was in a meeting recently, the 'Sasiwn' was here and there were reps from each church and we were organising it and it was 'will the ladies of so and so make the tea and we'll have to have a crowd of men to organise the parking' and I put my hand up and said 'I'd like to help organise the parking' and people looked, 'oh, ok Marged'. But I was trying to make the point. Why can't I help with the parking if I want to?! There's still that attitude within chapel life as opposed to secular life.

She recounts other occasions where she has herself been stereotyped as a troublemaker, standing up for the rights of women:

> Every time I speak about something, on the rights of women, they go 'oh yeah … you!' I remember when the vicar here teased me at a Bible study, one of the prophets where they put a woman in container and roll her down the road or something, I don't remember and he said 'oh you'll like this bit won't you!' He knows my standpoint. So I said, 'Well, you finish it and then I'll say my piece!' It's just the images of women in religion.

She referred to herself, in a jokey manner, as a 'freak' several times in her interview and it was interesting that she felt she was the one portrayed as the fanatic because it is known that she would object to the idea of a woman being put in a container and rolled down a road. In her minister's 'fraternal' misogyny was joked about, and Marged's feminism and desire to see both women and men treated with respect and justice was seen as abnormal. Marged demonstrated groundedness and confidence in that she was able to hold her own and refused to feel shamed or to submit to the dominant view. She did this with humour as well as resilience.

Harriet regarded her confidence as hard-won and only something she had achieved fairly recently, and ascribed it to her relationship with the divine. Although she had been describing how she had felt rejected by the church, she explored with me how this experience of alienation had been both fruitful and creative. She did not accept how she had been treated but had come to accept herself and a new role, and she attributed this to her relationship with God. This God, she believed, did not want her to sacrifice herself but to 'live life to the full'.

Lucy explored agency in terms of the institutional church and in particular the Church in Wales, which she considered as having a higher sense of its own agency because of disestablishment:

Probably we're not afraid to try new things. It's one thing in the Church in Wales, perhaps that's come out of that.

We're the … entrepreneurial, oh I'm not going to say that, we're the …

MANON: Pioneers?

LUCY: … Because that was a very brave step to take at the time without knowing how that was going to affect the church within the Principality so it has probably and maybe the freedom, we've had it more so than people in Scotland or England, we've been allowed to develop our identity alongside people of other faiths in Wales and haven't been afraid or seen other faiths as a threat but have seen how we can work alongside them.

It was during this discussion that she casually mentioned women as being 'stronger'. Although she seemed to regard this statement as controversial and problematic (her embarrassed laughter seemed to indicate this) her argument was that, as homemakers in the twentieth century and as those left behind during the war years, women had safeguarded the Christian values of home and community. This portrayal chimed with that of the stereotype of the Welsh Mam: 'If the father had been out at work all day and working away, the person who would have been really displaying the Christian values would have been the mother.'

In terms of her own faith and its influences on her life, she regarded this as wholly positive, despite listing some difficult experiences of dealing with the church and other Christian institutions. She commented that her 'sense of self-worth and value would, yes, emanate from my perception of my faith'. However, during the time of her parents' divorce she felt let down pastorally by the church and later in her working life, when working for a Christian organisation, she was on the receiving end of what she considered to be deeply unchristian behaviour. However, this did not shake her confidence in herself, or in the confidence and high self-esteem which her faith instilled in her:

I think, I feel that my faith underpins who I am and what I am and I hope that I try and act in an honourable way. I'm not saying I am perfect because I know I am not by a long shot. But I try and I think my faith underpins the actions that I take and decisions that I make so … it's a support, my faith stands by me and allows me to be the person that I am. It's like having a sense of gentle direction, almost like a support that underpins or deals with things life throws at you. So it definitely has been a positive and is a positive because it allows me to see myself and how I relate to other people.

Her own agency was also reflected in the recurring theme of this interview, that Welsh women were 'strong'. Her response when I asked more about this was:

Yes, I think we are strong. I think we are independent, I think we are opinionated but in a good way … I think we have an identity that there is an underlying strength within the community which owes in no small part to the women within it: I think Welsh women are strong. I think we've had to be! Without being too stereotypical in mining communities and how we've evolved when men have gone down to the pit, women have been left with a lot of responsibility, you've got a husband who may not come home and he's your main breadwinner so what are you going to do then? We've never been afraid to stand up and be counted. I think Welsh women are strong breed of … game old birds!

This contradicted my initial thesis that Welsh women have a stigmatised identity and feel oppressed. In fact several of the women spoke about women as strong and resilient, and in particular related it to motherhood and the stereotype of the Welsh Mam.

Mothering, being mothered and the role of women

I was surprised that the issue of mothering was so important for my participants. Sera and Elinor referred to their own mothers as their heroes (unprompted). Although Bethan and Elinor had felt restricted and socialised by their own mothers into behaving respectably, they also spoke about the importance they assigned to their own mothering in helping their own children grow up with strong moral values, as did Stefania, Lucy and Helen.

Several women reported that their own mothers had given them ambivalent messages about their place in the world. Elinor discussed how her (grand)mother had reminded her that women did not 'know their own minds' until they were in their thirties and cautioned against early marriage, as she herself had enjoyed the freedom that a career had given her in her twenties. Yet, in other ways, she had attempted to socialise Elinor into living a respectable life according to the expectations of the community. Elinor said about her:

> ... she was a woman born in the wrong generation – she really taught me the strength that women aren't meant to be at home looking after children, we are supposed to be out there in the world doing things ...

Likewise Marged's mother was very much her own person and did not see her role as simply that of a minister's wife:

> Mam was a minister's wife and took an interest but she wasn't the stereotype. She worked full-time and I remember her saying that when she got married, she was young and she said she was her own person and I'm not just a minister's wife. I think she'd said in her first chapel when she married at about twenty-four and we welcome Mrs Robert Jones and she said it's enough for me having taken on his surname, I don't want to take on his first name as well. My name is Mrs Elinor Jones!

However, despite running a thriving business, she expected her daughter to fulfil some traditional gender roles, for example she was horrified when Marged got up to make a speech at her own wedding and hissed at her to sit down.

The way the women worked out their mothering was radically different from previous generations. Marged and Stacey spoke about how gender roles are now different in the home compared to previous generations and they were critical of the expectation that women would fulfil most of the domestic chores, in church as well as in the home. Stacey said:

> Well Welsh women are known as ... the Mams aren't they, they're the ones who within the home they are in control of the home really and they see the men, their role is like ... I'm not referring to my role, my mother's generation and a bit younger, the women are the home-makers, they do everything for the men. The men can't possibly use any

appliances. They can't even … they can just about make a cup of tea but then that goes into church life that the men do all the practical things, the DIY, the hard labour stuff and they are seen as unmanly if they don't do that and if they do something more with the children, or more in the home then that's not right you know. You are like feminising them.

Marged regarded the different roles given to men and women as a product of the different generational expectations:

But the truth is, in the home, at my home, my husband cooks more than me really. We share much more, fifty-fifty though having said that I do all the ironing but I don't hoover. I'm quite proud of that. It's called Dad's hoover at home.

MANON: So is this a generational thing?

MARGED: Yes, I would think so, but Dad was quite good. Mam worked full time and he was at home so it would make sense for him to do the tea, but when I think of my in-laws, my father-in-law doesn't cook.

Marged also talked about Welsh women being strong and related this to Wales's industrial history – quarry life and rural communities.

Several expressed dissatisfaction with aspects of religion which seemed oppressive towards women: Jessie took exception to Christianity being about 'worshipping a man', Marged, Sera, Stefania and Lucy all spoke unprompted about the ministry of women and about the important symbolic significance of women being ministers, priests and bishops as a matter of justice. Furthermore, an important discourse for Marged was of rights, especially equal rights at work. She was proud of the record of her own Free Church denomination and heavily critical of the Free Church denomination she worked for on their maternity record and payment for lay workers as opposed to ordained ministers. More women were lay workers and more men ordained ministers, so she felt this was discriminatory on several levels.

The women I interviewed reflected shifting expectations of women, particularly in the complex roles and expectations ascribed to both them and their mothers. They were clear that they also wanted to lead fulfilling lives in their own right and not be tied to the demands of home and family as in previous generations. They were also critical of the sexism inherent in the churches and chapels, particularly in the assignment of gender roles, and found this aspect of church life alienating and out of step with their own world view or experience.

Narratives of resilience

In some of the interviews, the resilience of the women was demonstrated in the life stories themselves as well as in their comments. Strength and agency was not simply an aspiration or a world view, and two narratives in particular exemplified the resilience that some of the other participants had noted as being characteristic of Welsh women.

Hannah's interview recounted some difficult events in her life which she had worked hard to overcome. She had grown up in a north Walian coastal town, with an emotionally abusive and alcoholic mother who later turned to the Mormons for emotional support. Hannah herself was baptised by the local Mormon Church (which she found a 'terrifying experience'). As her siblings were older and her mother agoraphobic, Hannah found that she brought herself up as well as having to care for her mother.

At thirteen years of age Hannah was attacked, an experience she kept to herself for twenty years. When she was fifteen her mother left home and Hannah had to fend for herself, surviving by forging her mother's signature on her benefit book. She moved to Liverpool when she was sixteen after having met her future husband who was on a fishing trip in north Wales. They were married when she was twenty-three and went to church regularly; Hannah stated that she 'really enjoyed it' as it 'lifted her ... out of [her] ... life completely'.

In her twenty years with her ex-husband she suffered sustained emotional abuse:

> ... at some points when I was in Liverpool living with him if I went out of the house to see friends ... I didn't have any friends; he didn't want me to have any friends. I went out once and I came back and he had an air rifle and he put that to my head for two hours.

However, she remained with him for several years until he had an affair with a family friend. By that time she had become pregnant with her daughter, whom she considered the best thing that had ever happened to her.

She has been single now for over five years and is very happy – she enjoys her job and feels fulfilled by getting involved in raising money for charity. However, her ex-husband is now working in the same hospital as her and is often in touch, even at times propositioning her.

When she recounted her life events, which also included her mother's death when she was seventeen and a continuing relationship with her father (who may or may not be her biological father) I asked her what helped her deal with the difficulties of her unstable mother and abusive marriage. Her response was:

> I smile a lot and laugh. I just keep going, I think of people who've had worse experiences than me but I'm not the only one. And if what I go through makes me a stronger person I can help others who maybe can't cope with it as much.

She then talked about how her smile and positive nature is often commented on at work and how her charity work also helps her feel good about herself. Being helpful in turn helps her self-esteem, and being independent from her ex-husband (she does not receive any maintenance) also helps her feel empowered:

> I am getting stronger and stronger and stronger as a person. I'm getting confident of doing ... I feel that I could do anything that I wanted if I put my mind to it. I could do it. Yes, I would like to, I don't know, just if people came up with ... like you needed me to have a talk to you today, someone else came up to me and said I need this doing ... I would see if I can help somebody else out. Because it makes you feel better, you know, when you see someone who is down or fed up and you can bring a little bit of hope or a smile to them, it brightens your life up.

Helen's life story was similarly dramatic. Her parents divorced when she was young; they had had a volatile relationship. She attended Sunday school as a child but did not continue to attend, and at another stage in her childhood she had some input from the mother of a friend who was a Presbyterian but religion did not play a large part in her life.

She started working in the hotel industry and eventually moved to Manchester and then London to be near a boyfriend. When that relationship did not work out she moved back to north Wales, eventually meeting a new boyfriend, becoming pregnant and getting married (in the local Anglican church). She expressed some guilt about this sequence of events, as well as getting married in church when she was not a regular worshipper. She commented that it would not have felt right getting married anywhere else. She described church as a place to mark important events in life (sadly, she had experienced a stillbirth and her baby was buried in the graveyard there).

Her marriage failed: her husband gambled and was an alcoholic and the divorce again led her to feel guilty, especially because of her own experience as a child of divorced parents. However, despite all these traumatic events, which also included several miscarriages, she presented herself, as did Hannah, as someone who could face any difficult experience that life threw at her. Their resilient personas, however, did not utilise a personal faith; experience of religion was completely tangential to their lives.

Religion, belonging and alienation

If the women's confidence and self-image was ambivalent, so were their experiences of religion and of Welsh community life. Sera, for example, felt very much at home in her own chapel despite not being able to be completely open to everyone about her sexuality. This quote illustrates the ambivalence well:

> In a rural area like this, there is a strong sense of belonging. But you're never sure you can be completely yourself. If you don't fit the tidy normal pattern although that's not as strong as it used to be, lots of people with families who have split so it's not just the perfect nuclear family any more.

She described identity as formed in difference, as we can see in her description of how she felt about her own village, on one side of a valley. This was also related to religion and how they practised it, as well as class:

> This is an area ... this side of the valley is different in this part of the community, we don't take ourselves so seriously.

> MANON: So the other parts of the valley ...?

> SERA: More cultured [laughs]. There is more of a mix here, more down to earth on this side. The people who move in, the teachers and so on will move to the areas the other side. More professionals and so on. This is why I like my chapel, we can be ourselves, there is a spirit that's more ... compared to the chapel in the community the other side of the town. They are more narrow-minded. We're a chapel of rapscallions ...

Lucy spoke about feeling rooted in her community, with faith, Welshness, family and community all interweaving. For most of my participants, a sense of belonging was also related to national identity as well as to their community.

National identity

Some of my participants reported that they grew up feeling 'different', especially if they were not chapel and therefore not Welsh enough. Both Stefania and Bethan felt alienated for being Catholic. Bethan commented that she now went to chapel as it was 'more of a Welsh thing to do' and Stefania expressed powerfully the alienation arising from being dual heritage Italian and Welsh, and again not feeling that she belonged anywhere. For most of the sample, to be chapel was indeed to be more Welsh.

Stefania described her alienation arising from her dual heritage when she had moved to Italy as a young person:

> The first two years living in Italy I didn't form part of the expats. I didn't meet other British people, there weren't any other Welsh people to meet anyway and I didn't feel, I didn't identify with the English people so I didn't have any connections with them, but I went through a phase of feeling quite lonely so I went to the church in Venice …
>
> … I was just a nanny so I didn't fit in that way so the only person who would talk to me was another Italian and I just felt even though I'm in a Protestant church, Church of Wales, I don't know any of the songs, I couldn't do the Lord's Prayer in English, because I was used to doing it in Welsh and I just went away feeling quite empty. That somehow it hadn't filled the gap in the same way that I had expected it so I had to kind of find another way of making new friends and new connections.

For Stefania, denomination was a carrier of national identity: Catholicism was Italian and Church in Wales/Free Church, Welsh. She also contrasted the Welsh and Italian tendency to make connections between people and their community spirit with the greater formality of English people. However, she also regarded this community spirit as alienating and also affecting the church's ability to attract people. Younger people want more anonymity, not to be observed by those behind twitchy curtains or commented on by other members of the community.

Stefania illustrated how identity can be formed in opposition to other identities and the resulting alienation from not quite belonging to one or the other. However, she had successfully constructed a new identity for herself: she now appreciated the way in which her dual heritage had given her an appreciation and tolerance of different backgrounds and cultures as well as the Christianity from school and Sunday school which had shaped her as a child. These were values she wanted to pass to her son.

She regarded her dual heritage as something which made her more open-minded and non-judgemental. Her discussion of famous Welsh people again led to an interesting reflection on dual heritage, race and Welshness. She mentioned the presenter Jason Mohammed, and a programme where he had explored his Muslim and Welsh roots, saying that he couldn't separate out the Welsh and Muslim parts within his identity as they were integrated; this was also how Stefania felt.

She did not feel able to tick a white British box when having to decide on her own ethnic background. The categories did not match up to her experience. She regarded herself as being able to have a dual nationality (in terms of passports) but not 'two religions'. This was something I neglected to follow up; it would have been interesting to find out what stopped her from observing religion in the way she wanted to. She did not seem currently to be a regular attender of worship. For her religion and national identity were very closely linked.

Bethan's story revealed a tension and alienation that arose from being a Catholic in a Welsh-speaking family and community, against the background of the Troubles in Northern Ireland. As a child she was bullied for being Catholic and was unintentionally excluded from the Urdd competitions at school because the practice sessions for the Eisteddfod were held in the chapel, during Sunday school. When she had children of her own, even though she had married in a Catholic church, her husband persuaded her to have the children baptised in a chapel and for them to continue to attend on an *ad hoc* basis as going to chapel was more of a 'Welsh thing to do'. She agreed with this in part so that her children did not face the bullying and exclusion she herself had faced:

> There was a lot of talk at the time of the IRA and that kind of thing with Catholicism ...
> When they found out I went to church they could be quite nasty so to an extent I felt
> ashamed growing up being a Catholic ... To an extent, until I got married, I kept it
> quiet.

> But we got married in a Catholic church so people knew afterwards so when I was
> having children I wanted to raise them as Welsh chapel and I didn't want them to feel
> odd, as I felt as a child growing up, that they would be involved with Welsh culture and
> my husband, even though he didn't go to chapel or anything he had strong feelings that
> he didn't want them to be raised as Catholics and I didn't feel strongly enough the other
> way to object so ... that's why I take them to chapel so that they have really what I
> missed out on.

For Helen, religion was an important aspect of British rather than Welsh identity. She considered herself to be Welsh and not English, however her view of why Christianity was important seemed to be part of a wider discourse about British nationality and Christianity being inextricably linked, and about the 'dangers' of other faiths (particularly Islam) to a British way of life. She was the only person to express this view in my sample:

> British society really is breaking down and falling around our ears and we have lost our
> way in a lot of things and a lot of other religions are seeping in and we'll wake up one
> day wearing a burka you know which is all well and good for Muslim countries but the
> UK is a Christian country and I think perhaps at some point it's time we woke up and
> realised that at some point before it's too late really to be honest.

For Helen, Christianity was a carrier of British national identity and other religions carriers of other national identities. I found this statement uncomfortable, though similar discourses are part of the discussion about nationality and religion in Britain today, particularly within the media and politics.

Religion, for my research participants, had affected their sense of national identity in different ways and showed how this can lead to a sense of alienation, belonging or even an ambivalent experience.

Class

Class was also an issue in terms of whether the women felt they 'belonged' in their context. Most, though not all, of my participants would be considered middle-class and most were in professional jobs, but a complex picture emerged of how religion and class were linked. Marged and Jessie, living and working in a similar Welsh-speaking housing estate, spoke movingly of certain women who had not been able to fulfil their potential because of their class. Marged told the story of how the chapels in her own childhood were regarded as having different status and those from the estate would feel awkward about coming to the main chapel in town:

> Back in the thirties and forties a lot of the chapels had their own missions and you would have Sunday school for the town kids, but the ones here wouldn't be able to go up to the town chapel. [Laughs] So they felt … there is a story that in my own chapel when I was growing up the minister there said it was wrong, everyone needs to come up to the chapel and they stopped coming altogether then!

> MANON: So why couldn't they come to the chapel Sunday school?

> MARGED: Well before you would have the chapel upstairs and then the vestry downstairs and the town children would just come and the Sunday school was downstairs, but they couldn't go upstairs to the chapel itself, maybe because they were too scruffy, I don't know. When the new minister came in the sixties and changed things and said this isn't right, everyone has to come up to the chapel, so they stopped coming altogether then.

Jessie, Bethan and Sera spoke about a stereotype of a certain type of middle-class Welsh woman who goes to the eisteddfod, sings in choirs and looks down on other Welsh people, and they were passionately critical of the elitism and snobbery of the Welsh middle class. This was surprising given that they themselves could be considered to be part of this group potentially given their professions. However, they had been completely alienated by a group of people who, according to them, were superior and exclusive. Being 'chapel', according to Jessie, was part of this identity.

Jessie spoke about how this selfish (in her view) middle class had silenced others, hijacked the language and made it impossible for anyone to critique anything that is traditionally Welsh as irrelevant because we could be seen to be criticising the language itself:

> But we're not going to slam the harp, or slam the eisteddfod because they do so much to keep the language alive so that gags us from speaking about that Welsh middle class monster that goes from strength to strength.

Jessie lived on a housing estate and her response to my question about stereotypes of Welsh women was interesting and unexpected:

MANON: So tell me are there stereotypes of women in Wales?

JESSIE: Well a lot of women are beaten ... I see them outside school picking up their children, with black eyes. Is that a stereotype? In the Welsh-speaking Wales where I live yes, stereotypes, women ...

I failed to follow this up, but in the course of our conversation, not on tape, she also mentioned other women who had experienced and come through domestic abuse (this time from a middle-class background) and her immense admiration for them.

Jessie's estate has an unusually a high percentage of Welsh speakers. These people regard the middle class as *pobl fawr gachu* according to Jessie, literally the 'shitty big people', though she then commented that this is also how they see 'people who work and own a car'. However, these people she felt were alienated from Welsh-speaking Wales, especially the middle class who have:

... claimed the language and through that they trample on it and alienate people like this estate with its incredibly high percentage who speak Welsh. The ruling Welsh middle-class Welsh have alienated people on purpose I believe. They don't use clear and understandable Welsh – to keep people out. They want it to be elitist. There is a way of including people. But they've gone out of their way to alienate and keep people out, because we only want our type of person involved.

You see it now with the eisteddfod, the group raising money for the *Urdd* eisteddfod coming here. They are very happy in their own company. They don't try and include people, but that's what managers/the ruling class are like. They exclude people, keep the proletariat [*gwerin*] out. It's not natural it is new and has happened insidiously. (Laughs). Class war!! That's what we need in Wales!

Jessie was very politically informed and her lively views were original and perceptive. This form of critique of the Welsh ruling class in my experience is something which is often alluded to in private or in jokes, but not publicly acknowledged. Her phrase 'Plaid Cymru Methodists' to my knowledge is unique to her.

Bethan was also aware of the stereotype of women who go to the eisteddfod 'all grand and thinking they are someone' so like Jessie she was critical of the Welsh middle class and reported that she had written a satirical piece at college describing this type of woman:

At college I had to write something for a language course, what we wanted to do in the future and how we saw ourselves in ten years and I wrote completely tongue in cheek I want to be the mother of however many children and I want to own a Volvo, big enough to carry a harp, go to eisteddfodau in a caravan and I wanted to be in a Cerdd Dant choir wearing a Laura Ashley dress ... He marked me down because he didn't believe I wanted to be like Mam, he hadn't realised I was being totally sarcastic. I guess we wouldn't wear Laura Ashley dresses now; it would be linen trousers and a long top to the floor but for me that's the stereotypical Welsh woman by now. People who go to eisteddfodau all grand and thinking they are someone but it is nothing like me ...

This mythical person Bethan regarded as very much a chapel and not church (particularly Roman Catholic) attender. She was also critical of the hypocrisy she had seen in both churches and chapels, people who 'are actually quite unpleasant people'.

In Sera's interview, various Welsh identities were held in tension; she contrasted herself and others with the *cyfryngis* and *pobl y pethe*, that is, the Welsh-speaking, literary, eisteddfod, media types who actually repulse her (she made a gesture of being physically sick when I asked her if she fitted in to this category!)

Discourses of identity, class and Welshness were evident in these research conversations and some of the participants, such as Sera, would speak about identity in terms of difference. One of the characteristics of the *cyfryngis/pobl y pethe* is that they see themselves as part of the *gwerin* i.e. a romanticised working class even though they have a high level of income and are in professional jobs. Sera, Bethan and Jessie felt that this was disingenuous. Although critical of this social grouping, they were not unhappy that they felt alienated by them as they did not want to be seen as part of them. The discussion about stereotypes and archetypes is a significant one when discussing my participants' identities and therefore I now turn to discussing the question of who were the role models and heroines of the participants. This yielded a particularly fruitful discussion about Welsh women's identity and self-perceptions and further discussions about class and race.

Stereotypes, archetypes and role models

There was a huge variety in responses when I asked participants to discuss stereotypes, role models and famous Welsh women. Most of the women felt uncomfortable with the question and expressed shame at their lack of knowledge. It also led to conversations about narratives and how stories are used to shape our thinking. Elinor mentioned Mary Jones, who walked barefoot to Bala to buy a Bible, inspiring the Bible Society. Yet, Jessie was critical of how this story had been used to glorify poverty. Hannah mentioned Betsi Cadwaladr, a nurse at around the same time as Florence Nightingale. (The local health authority board had recently been named after her.) Lucy spoke about her as well as Mary Seacole, commenting that until recently her story had not been told because she was black. Some of the women were aware of the power of story and were critical of how stories are used by those in power.

Several politicians were mentioned in response to the question – Leanne Wood (recently elected leader of Plaid Cymru during the time of the conversations), Sian Howys, Julie Morgan, Helen Mary Jones and the writers, Menna Elfyn, Mererid Hopwood and Bethan Gwanas. Some comedic characters were mentioned – Ruth Madoc in *Hi de Hi* and Nessa (played by Ruth Jones) from *Gavin and Stacey*. Others mentioned women clergy or Christian leaders who had inspired them. People could immediately think of singers, for example Shirley Bassey, but were self-critical of this, as fulfilling a stereotype of Welsh people being good singers.

This led Stefania to discuss race:

> Yes, I used to do Welsh awareness training for the agency that I worked with before. I'd
> have to go to groups in England and I would have pictures of people or scenery or facts
> and they would have to choose one and talk about why they had chosen that particular
> image. Whenever I went to London they would always argue, you haven't got enough
> black people. And I thought I can only think of one black Welsh person, a female and
> that was Shirley Bassey. She stood out.

Race is not something that was discussed often amongst my interviewees and all
of them were white (though Stefania identified herself as dual heritage Italian–
Welsh and olive-skinned, not white). However Bassey does not conform to the
stereotype of the Welsh Mam, white and chapel going: one of the most famous
Welsh women has very little impact on general stereotypes of Welsh women.

Religion featured in this discussion and it was acknowledged, as Beddoe has
commented, that many famous Welsh women were religious (Beddoe in Curtis,
1986: 232), and that this formed an important part of the stereotype of Welsh
women generally. As I have already mentioned, Elinor commented that she
regarded the chapel-going woman as a salient Welsh stereotype, as stricter and
more judgemental as opposed to churchgoers who were more 'laid-back'. My
participants' responses seem to suggest that religious women do have an 'image
problem' and that this is particularly true for Nonconformist women. Whilst all
the churchgoing women in my sample rejected this persona, it seemed a genuine
and influential archetype linked to the previous generation.

When I asked Hannah the question about characteristics and stereotypes of
Welsh women she also thought of Welsh women as strong, though she was aware
that others had a negative view of this strength, as an aggressiveness and a refusal
to speak English to others. However, her view was that Welsh women were kind
as well as confident:

> People say to me who would I choose for a team – of English, Scottish or Irish women
> or Welsh women, then it would be Welsh women because they are determined and
> they've got something different. I don't know, it's culture, but we're proud to be who
> we are and why should we be quiet and not show you know what sort of women we are
> because everybody else does, so I don't see why we don't.

Jinny regarded the Welsh stereotypes in the media as from south rather than north
Wales, and also believed that the small communities in northern England would
be 'exactly the same' as the small communities in north Wales. She clearly was
familiar with the stereotype of Welsh people as being emotional or sentimental,
particularly about nationhood and rugby. Interestingly, she was ambivalent about
essentialism, at times speaking about each person being unique and there being
no difference between men and women, as well as joking about hormones making
her emotional.

The women were aware of the stereotypes of women in Wales, as well as critical of who gets to decide whose story is told and which story is influential. The
most significant aspect of this part of the interview was how embarrassed many of
them felt when they found it difficult to name Welsh heroines or role models, as
well as the fact that several of them named their own mothers.

Spirituality, values and nostalgia

The experience and outlook of those identifying as non-religious

Out of my sample, two women were non-religious, Jinny and Jessie. Both were Welsh-speaking and were reacting against conservative forms of Christianity which they felt were oppressive and harmful. Although they were comfortable in their own non-faith, they also regarded their experience as unusual and to some extent marginalised. Jessie, in particular, commented that she had had an unusually secular upbringing. Both spoke about the boredom of their experiences of church or chapel worship. Jinny found her sister's faith as a 'born-again Christian' infantile, and her attempts to speak to Jinny about her faith tedious and inappropriate. It was also barrier to Jessie that God was perceived as male, as was Jesus ('worshipping a man!') and that religion promises 'pie in the sky when you die' leading those who are oppressed to simply accept their situation in life.

However Jessie stressed that she was a spiritual person – though this was expressed in her ethics and values rather than through any practices or experiences of the divine. She had researched creation from a scientific and a religious point of view and had come to the conclusion that 'there must be something somewhere. But I don't know what. If I did, I would be very clever!' Jessie expressed some interest in Buddhism but didn't consider herself a 'good enough person' to follow that path. She was more interested in politics and nationality, though was very critical of a nationalist agenda which she felt was elitist.

For Jinny, religion was something that elderly people were interested in and belonged in the past. For her, the internet and globalisation had transformed Welsh culture and way of life, and that religion had no place in modern Wales. However, she did not think that faith would dwindle and die, she pointed to the example of her evangelical sister as evidence that newer forms of faith would come to take the place of traditional churchgoing.

Jinny and Jessie spoke of the hypocrisy of religion, of someone going to chapel on a Sunday and beating their spouse, or having an affair during the week. However, both were also envious of the comfort that religion seemed to bring others. Jinny seemed to consider all the denominations as being similar, yet Jessie was very critical of the Calvinistic Methodists in particular and their alignment with the Welsh ruling class. Both Jessie and Jinny were clear that their non-religion was a choice and one based on their own moral values. Both attempted to lead lives which were in accordance with values of tolerance, care for others and concern for the oppressed.

Jinny was unique amongst my participants in not wanting to elaborate on her story and very quickly, in response to a question from me about the effect of religion on her life, spoke about chapel as 'boring' and religion as damaging:

> I'm not unspiritual. But I am irreligious. I have a belief, but no religion, if that makes sense. Religion is one of the worst things in the world. It has caused so many wars and fighting that anything else is better. Well, in my opinion, everyone has a right to their opinion.

She spoke about religion being just like supporting a football team, or worshipping 'Captain Kirk rather than Mr Spock'. Her attitude towards difference was to be accepting, characterised maybe by a 'live and let live' approach, though when I conveyed this to her she agreed, then said, in language laden with religious imagery: 'Yes, that's very important, for everyone. Well, no, not paedophiles. I draw a line at them. They need to go to hell in little pieces.' She spoke in evolutionary terms about the progress of liberal values, or 'tolerance' as she put it – women being accepted into the ministry and Wales being more of an open-minded nation now, something she ascribed to the internet and television, the broadening of our cultural horizons. Religion was seen by her as part of the heritage but not of the future of Wales. She saw a relative's faith as a sign of weakness, whereas she did not need religion as she had a 'hardness maybe, a switch – it's in our family – that we don't feel things very deeply'.

Jinny's view reflected a secularist discourse that regards religion as both irrelevant and dangerous in the modern world and believes that those who practise Christianity are often hypocritical. For Jinny, religion was a negative influence, not particularly on Welsh culture but on Western culture as a whole. Village and industrial life had shaped the people of Wales but no more than any other nation within Britain. Her view of Welsh women was unashamedly non-essentialist. Religion was boring and would be superseded by rationalism.

Christian Values

Given that my sample was largely friends and acquaintances and others found through a snowball approach and through social media, my sample was unusually religious. However, amongst the women who identified as Christian, the role of nostalgia was strong, as was the sense that religion was part of the past, and part of an identity rooted in Wales. Lucy commented:

> I think the Welsh [Christian values] definitely [are] about the family, taking care of the family, the extended family, the responsibility we see quite strongly within our threads of family. And also how we treat other people. You treat other people how you want to be treated yourself. There is a respect within the community to yourself and to other people and to their possessions, and perhaps in some ways it would be perceived as quite old fashioned … It goes back to that community [idea], people looked out for another, we've lost that idea haven't we.

For Stefania, certain practices such as celebrating Epiphany were very important to her as part of her Italian heritage, and her family Bible, where the names of all the children in the family were inscribed, was an important part of her Welsh identity.

Given my age profile, it wasn't unexpected that the research participants mentioned baptism and marriage in particular. For Lucy, marriage and a sense of duty in wanting to attend the church where she was going to get married led her to return to the religious practice that had been encouraged in her as a child. Helen also felt guilty for 'using' the church for her wedding and the baptism of her child, and expressed some awkwardness that her child had been born out of wedlock and baptised before their marriage. Helen is not a regular churchgoer and is not sure of her present commitment to Christianity but was aware of a church influence on her life:

> Because in society, really it's more acceptable to be married first in the eyes of the Church and to have children within marriage and although I'm not particularly a churchgoer, as such, I do have strong values. So for me it wasn't ideal really that situation was that way, but it happened – and to hell with it!

> Yes, so we got married and again I suppose again you could say that it was perhaps a little hypocritical that we got married in a church, because neither of us went to church. But it wouldn't have felt right getting married anywhere else and again I'm not quite sure why that would be. Maybe it's something that's drummed into you from a young age. Maybe it's just a pattern that you're supposed to do, but for me it wouldn't have felt right getting married in a hotel or you know, on a cliff top or I felt, I wanted it to be in a church.

For Stefania, her values were very important and part of her spirituality and Christian background. This could be characterised as a non-judgemental attitude and cultural relativism. She was also very much in favour of teaching religion to children as it was important to teach them morality from a religious standpoint.

Bethan also held values to be important even though she was not a regular attender at her chapel. She was, in fact, grateful for the rather strict Roman Catholic moral upbringing which had instilled values in her, though she questioned the hypocrisy of some in church and also whether you had to go to church to be a Christian: 'I think it's to do with the way people live their lives every day which makes them more of a Christian than someone who sits in chapel every Sunday listening to you talking.' This reflected several other comments that my participants made: hypocrisy and bad behaviour within the churches was criticised severely and had had an impact on their attitudes towards the churches.

Lucy's values of treating others as you would like to be treated were similar to Jinny's, and she went on to describe her Lenten discipline of conducting a daily anonymous act of kindness, which she ascribed to her Christian faith. Like Jinny she felt that the small close-knit communities were what made Welsh communities hold certain values, such as kindness, in common. In fact several of the participants mentioned rurality, industries such as coal mining, quarrying or farming as having had a marked influence on the identity of Welsh people, especially women.

Nostalgia and the symbolic significance of social spaces

Many of the women still saw Wales's industrial heritage as something which shaped perceptions of Welshness and of the different roles and pressures on men and women. The pit, the quarry and rurality were all seen as places where roles have been enacted and still affect behaviours. For example, the stereotype of the Welsh Mam, running the home while the father was down the pit or in the quarry still had resonance and contributed to women's perception of themselves.

Lucy was the person who expressed this most strongly, claiming that Welsh women have always had to be strong in order to cope with this difficult way of life. Lucy showed how, in her world view, social space had shaped Welsh identity, with the pit and the home influencing certain roles for men and women in industrial Wales. The archetype of the Welsh Strong Woman in the home and the man working down the pit had significance for her even though this was far removed from her own experience, or that of her family.

The other space that had affected women's lives according to my sample was rural village life. Small, bounded communities had contributed to strong and intimate relationships and in some ways these had been detrimental to women and their socialising into certain respectable patterns of behaviour, as well as policing them and inculcating shame if they transgressed, for example in falling pregnant out of wedlock.

This sense of shame could also be seen in other aspects of village life, for example, Sera reporting that members of the community simply felt too embarrassed to start attending chapel after a long period of non-attendance as they would become a talking point for others. For her, village life hindered as well as helped a sense of belonging. The internet, however, had made a huge difference to her and she regarded this as the main reason she did not feel isolated or need to move to an area with more gay people to feel more accepted.

Jinny also mentioned the internet as having changed the Welsh rural way of life completely with virtual spaces changing the way people relate to one another. Globalisation meant that people had more in common than ever, and as such she would not accept there were differences between Welsh people and any other nationality.

The effect of social spaces (and virtual space) on the life of the women and their ability to form identity, and their significance within the women's figured worlds of Welshness surprised me. Even though none of my participants had ever worked in a mine or quarry, and, as far as I know, neither had any member of their families, the pit and quarry had meaning for them as part of their Welsh figured world. Buildings and artefacts can play an important part in constructing individual and social identity (Hurdley, 2013) and 'things' can also be imbued with emotion and meaning (Pattison, 2007). Nostalgia, as a bittersweet emotion, is an important aspect of self-identity (Dickinson and Erben, 2006) and an important part of Welsh national identity (Trosset, 1993: 152–3). Social spaces also have a symbolic significance (Lefebvre, 1991) and for my participants, the part that social spaces and nostalgia played in constructing Welsh identity was important.

Summary

The research conversations with these thirteen women challenged my initial perception that Welsh women lacked confidence or had a stigmatised identity. However, the discourse of respectability and repression was one which had relevance to them, had featured in their upbringing and was linked to religion. This was particularly a perception of a chapel culture which was part of their Welsh figured worlds, whatever denomination or religious upbringing they had

73

themselves received. Religion was seen as a carrier of Welsh identity, especially in its Free Church form.

However, the pressure to be respectable and not become a talking point had had little effect on the women; they had rebelled against it. They were certainly not socialising their own children into this same fear of 'what Mrs Jones down the road would say'. The direct link they made between chapel culture and repression is possibly not unique to Wales although as the literature shows, this is seen as characteristically Welsh within discourses of Welsh national identity. These conversations revealed a culture that is in a state of flux – the values and practices of the older generation were not being transmitted by them into the next generation. Even if the identity created for women as a result of the backlash against the Blue Books report had been operative for several generations, this study shows that it is no longer an identity that middle-aged women, and those following them, want to utilise for themselves.

The women told stories of how institutional religion and local church experiences could be misogynistic and oppressive and also how local churches, and especially personal faith, could be empowering and supportive. Resilience was not linked to religious beliefs. Although some women ascribed their high sense of self-esteem to their own relationship with the divine (but never institutional religion), similarly, the non-religious or occasional churchgoers were also agentic and resilient.

Several mentioned the archetype of the Strong Woman, linked to the Welsh Mam, as a particularly Welsh stereotype, and this seemed operative within their world view. This trope seemed more linked to Wales's industrial heritage than religion – the woman running the home while her husband was at the quarry or down the coal mine. The women's life stories exemplified this strength and resilience and I was impressed with the courage of the women who had faced difficult circumstances, even tragedy and abuse, and had not only withstood these difficulties but had overcome them and used them for their own development and in order to help others.

According to Castells's (2010) schema it could be argued that the women demonstrated a resistance identity, proud of their national identity and able to withstand the dominant discourses of Britishness and Englishness as well as the pressure to perform respectability. They had incorporated a new morality and other values derived from Christian tradition (even if they did not identify as Christians) but also (apart from in Helen's case) a commitment to the dominant discourses of equality and multiculturalism. The women felt comfortable in utilising what they found helpful in the Christian traditions and discarding the rest. Another feature of this resistance identity was humour – particularly in the conversations with Stacey, Jessie and Marged.

In order to understand whether these themes were also reflected in the lives of other women in Wales, instead of conducting further interviews I decided to triangulate the findings through looking at Welsh women's writing. Do similar themes emerge by looking at religion in the writings of women in current publication in their performance of identity?

6

Welsh Identity and Religion in Women's Writing

Writing was, and still is, for me ... akin to a spiritual experience.
(Elfyn in Aaron, Rees, Betts and Vincentelli, 1994: 281)

A fruitful space: insights from literature

Analysing records, writings and other cultural artefacts in historical research is common (Reinharz, 1992: 146). Within the discipline of Welsh studies it is also usual to gain insights about Welsh experience and identity from reflecting on Wales's literature, for example, Williams in his introduction to his book *Wales Unchained* comments that it is written:

> ... in the belief that 'literature' is a specific activity, but one in which the whole history of a culture is deeply inscribed and which is often ignored by historians and political scientists. (Williams, 2015: 336)

If literature has been ignored by some academic fields, it has been highly influential within feminist theology. Walton suggests that the boundary between literature and theology can be a fruitful space where difficult experiences and meaning-making can be explored (Walton, 2007: 35). Literature has provided a parallel set of sacred texts for women (Llewellyn, 2015: 10), and certainly one of the most influential writings within feminist or rather womanist thought has been a work of fiction – Alice Walker's *The Color Purple* (Walton, 2007: 8), a book which has also inspired Welsh women.

Literature, particularly poetry, has given Welsh women a voice to talk about their identity and religion, denied to them by traditional forms of theology: it could be argued that literature is where Welsh women have done their theology. In fact, there has been a lively and long tradition of women writing poetry in Wales since the fifteenth century, even if publicly, poetry has been dominated by men (Gramich and Brennan, 2003: xvii; Elfyn, 1991: v). Religion has been a significant theme within these writings, with the coexistence of erotic and devotional themes often in the same poem, as we have seen in the work of Gwerful Mechain (Gramich and Brennan, 2003: xvii).

In Chapter 4 in my discussion of images of Welsh women I have already mentioned the influential trope of the Welsh Mam in *How Green Was My Valley*, and the poetry of Gwerful Mechain in counterpoint; the dissonance between them had, in part, led me to research this question of how religion impacts the identity of Welsh women. Therefore, the next set of voices in this conversation is that of women writers, in memoir and poetry. I have chosen these women because their work is seen as significant or that their identities bring an added dimension into the conversation. My first conversation partner is Menna Elfyn, considered to be one of the most prominent female voices in Welsh language poetry at the end of the twentieth century (Gramich, 2007: 150–1).

Menna Elfyn: 'If Christ came back today he'd definitely be making his own cup of tea'

Elfyn is considered to be the 'best known Welsh language poet internationally'[23] and is the most published female writer working through the medium of Welsh (Elfyn, 2010: 4). She is a language activist and campaigner and has been imprisoned twice for non-violent protest and has brought 'a radical wave of feminism into traditional Welsh society' (Gramich, 2007: 153) through her writing. She comments in an interview on her own website:

> I came out of prison a feminist as I realised that many of the women there had no language at all or rather that they would find themselves unable to articulate their lives and their dreams for a better future.[24]

Her work has been translated into several languages, above all English, and she has travelled and performed widely. However, the fact that her work has been translated has caused controversy and it has been suggested that she has had to seek other avenues and audiences for her work because of her 'ostracisation' by the exclusive male club of Welsh poets (Hallam, 2010). Lloyd-Morgan comments that she is unaware of any other poet who has been as influential as Elfyn in articulating Welsh women's experiences (in Marks, 2013: 6). However Marks (2013) comments that there is very little exploration of her work, and Marks's own treatment in an epistolary book-length literary critical work is the only sustained examination of Elfyn's poetry apart from brief book chapters or journal articles.

In my study of her work I found that confidence/agency, religion/faith and language/voice are important themes. Elfyn reports that she was a shy child, unwilling to speak at the family dinner table, and had a speech impediment which affected her confidence (Elfyn, 2010: 5, 6). This struggle to find a voice and agency has been significant in her development as a feminist and Aaron (1997) comments that she has become 'the recognised spokeswoman of Welsh language feminist protest', quoting the following poem to evidence this, a poem which explores gaining agency as a woman through the process of growing up:

> I was humbly feminine
> now I am bold,
> I was spinelessly girlish
> now I am strong,
> I was powerlessly passive

> like my voiceless sex,
> I was contentedly restless
> through the centuries of rape.
> > But,
> > > watch
> > > > your
> > > > > step,
> > > > > > brother!

(Elfyn in Aaron, 1997, Aaron's own translation)

Elfyn's feminism has been informed by the work of the French feminists, particularly Hélène Cixous, and she sees gender as performative not essential, though she acknowledges the dilemma that in order to overturn inequality it has been necessary initially to stress gender differences (Elfyn, 1991: vi). She does not consider there to be a definitive female mindset and although there are experiences that are characteristically female, for example birth, menstruation and hysterectomies, she maintains that there is no such thing as male writing or female writing, or writing that is characteristic of a particular nation. It has been patriarchy which has attempted to restrict women and their identities by imposing the tropes of Eve/Mary on them (Elfyn, 1991: v).

Elfyn: religion

The reference to these religious figures could indicate that Elfyn sees religion as central to female oppression. However, her treatment of religion and faith is more complex. M. Wynn Thomas says about her that she has an 'ambivalent relationship to [that] Nonconformist culture which is apparent in all her writing'.[25] Although her entry in the *Cambridge Companion to Women's Writing in English* states that 'religion dances under the surface of her work' (Morley, 1999: 218) she herself does not refer to religion as a major theme in her own work, because for a PhD by publication, she identified Wales, children (and motherhood), women, people and places as her major areas of exploration (Elfyn, 2010: 3).

In her work there are echoes of the two dominant Christian traditions, the liturgical tradition of Anglicanism and Catholicism and the Nonconformist tradition, and this is often related to agency, voice and discourse. There are also some references to Eastern religious traditions. In the poem *Hymn to a Welshman*, a priest is the one 'who read the Word / on their behalf', rendering the nation passive, however the 'voiceless' and 'hoarse-voiced choir' of the spokesperson for the Welsh is a 'poet' (Elfyn, 2007: 225–6). Likewise, religion and freedom–captivity are important themes and the central character of her volume *Cell Angel* again reveals this ambivalence in Elfyn's treatment of religion:

> ... her cell is not just a prison – Elfyn has twice been imprisoned as a result of nationalist protest – but also a place for contemplation, while her angel is both Eastern and Christian. (Morley, 1999: 8)

God in Elfyn's prison in *Psalm to the Little Gap in the Cell Door* (Elfyn, 1996: 25) is not the Christian God of her upbringing but the earth goddess Gaia, whose eye is the eye-hole in the prison door, where different women look at her as the prisoner in the cell and she looks at them recognising the divine in them, prisoner and prison officer alike, this common humanity (and divinity) giving her a sense of freedom, an 'open door'.

Elfyn's father was a Congregationalist minister and there is reference to this in her poem *The Small Communion* (Elfyn, 2007: 167), where she describes the act of playing with his home communion set ('he was the only man I knew had a little set of cups without handles, who played at houses'). This poem is partnered with another, called *The Big Communion* (Elfyn, 2007: 169), in which she describes a church service at HMP Pucklechurch and her incredulity at the simplistic teaching and insensitivity of the priest:

> He gave out
>
> to them that God was not like a one-armed bandit
> in an arcade. Seriously, that's what he said.
>
> He was pretty brusque. 'Don't expect
> to put money in and hit the handy jackpot
>
> as you offer a prayer.' (Elfyn, 2007: 169)

Later, she describes how they were all on their knees 'not expecting anything – / nothing at all. / That's what he said wasn't it?' (Elfyn, 2007: 169). Humorously, she comments in her notes in *Perffaith Nam/Perfect Blemish* that the large crowd at the prison for communion 'may have something to do with the wine' (Elfyn, 2007: 295).

The title poem of *Cell Angel* (1996) reflects her experience of meeting a young male prisoner and she contrasts him with the other young men who perform in choirs in large churches: 'God's no more there / then here, in the angel cell.' (Elfyn, 1996: 21)

If a prison cell can be a confusing place, of contemplation and freedom as well as restriction and captivity, her poems about chapel buildings and life are more unambiguously critical (as a 'patriarchal institution', Marks, 2013: 217). In her two significant satirical poems about chapels, one pokes fun at the Welsh obsession with cleanliness being next to godliness and the other is a poem which satirises the discourse of women being asked to 'stay behind' to make the tea.

In *Cleaning the Chapel* (2007: 171), Elfyn elaborates on a comment the minister Eifion Powell made once in a sermon, that a chapel member had translated *Holy Spirit* in the English into 'Clean Spirit' in Welsh (Elfyn, 2007: 295). The poem suggests affectionately but humorously that the Welsh, unlike other 'saints' turning to 'sackcloth and ashes', had a much more clean attitude to religion 'stripping down to the skin / to wash, bathe and sing / in baths they called chapels' (2007: 171). The poem is resonant with the values of Welsh respectability and of the role of the woman in keeping a clean house – the Spirit like a 'charwoman armed with a duster' (2007: 171). Ironically, when I discussed this poem at an away day with the Welsh-speaking Methodist Synod's ministers, one participant failed to see the satire, commenting that 'clean' spirit was indeed an accurate and even better translation than 'holy'.

Will the Ladies Please Stay Behind (Elfyn, 1995: 17) is angrier and less affectionate in tone. She names and critiques the damaging assumptions and its 'will the ladies please stay behind' discourse of male leadership and female service within church life. It represents a call for women to stand up to the men who are making them 'stay behind' and restrict their own faith and leadership. She contrasts the voicelessness of the women in the present with the hope of speaking a new liturgy which is about standing up for ourselves and even challenging Christ himself.

WILL THE LADIES PLEASE STAY BEHIND?

A service.
Us in the sheepfold.
The deacons ranked, facing us,
bald, thoughtful.
Him in the pulpit says,
'Thanks to the women
    who served…'
Yes, served at the grave,
    wept, by the cross…
'And will the ladies' – the women –
    'please
        stay behind?'

Behind –
we're still behind,
still waiting,
serving,
smiling…still dumb…
the same two thousand years ago
    as today.

But the next time they say it
from the seat too big for women,
'Will the ladies, etc.'
what about singing out (all together now!)
in a chant, a new psalm,
a lesson being recited –

'Listen here, little masters,
if Christ came back today

he'd definitely be making
    His own cup of tea.' (Elfyn, 1995: 17)

Elfyn satirises Welsh religion, particularly chapel life, effectively and uses a variety of methods in order to critique the patriarchy of Wales's religious institutions. In this she has been a significant voice challenging the dominant patriarchal discourses of the churches in Wales and is an example of how poetry can critique and empower.

Elfyn: liturgy, voice and voicelessness

Liturgy is a key theme in Elfyn's work and one which has not received much attention. Often, as in the above poem, it is linked to voice and agency and is offered as a dissenting discourse. Several of her poems have liturgical names, particularly in translation, for example *Matins, Litany on the Beginning of a Burial, In Praise of the Moon* (Elfyn, 2007) as well as the poems already mentioned – though this may be an English influence, as the Welsh names for these poems are less liturgical in style.

In the poem *Song of a Voiceless Person to British Telecom* (Elfyn, 1995: 7, 9), translated by R. S. Thomas, liturgy is again used as a form of discourse. When the poet is told to 'speak up' when she speaks in Welsh to a BT call handler, she realises that the request is actually for her to speak in English and not in Welsh. She reflects on this and her voicelessness:

> No pronunciation, no annunciation,
> inflection. I am infected
> with dumbness. I can neither lampoon,
> sing in tune; much less can I
> intone. My grace-notes
> are neither music nor mumble.
> I am not heard at Evening Prayer
> nor at triumphal Matins. (1995: 7)

Welsh speakers have been rendered 'mutes, Trappists' (Elfyn, 1995: 7). However, she decides next time this happens that she will instead ask the operator to 'pipe down' and will comment that his words are like 'sounding brass', from 1 Corinthians 13. In one of her early poems, *Angladd*[26] (1978: 38), she expresses the pain of not being able to mark the death of her miscarried baby through ritual (Marks 2013: 91) and feels this is a form of silencing, though the poet eventually finds a voice to eulogise the lost baby in the second stanza (Elfyn, 1978: 38).

Her volume *Murmur* (2012) also contains several allusions to liturgy and services. For example, the collection opens with the poem *Ghazal: Loss* (Elfyn, 2012: 11) which is situated at a gravestone, described as an 'altar / of this tearful stone'; and the next poem, *Babysitting in the Crematorium* (2012: 13), also has loss and ritual as a theme but with an element of hope in the timelessness of a child's sleep. A 'found' poem, *Visitor* (Elfyn, 2012: 57), recounts the conversation of a relative who tells the story of a couple found making love in the chapel gallery during a communion service ('Think of the cheek of it – / we always keep the place unlocked, / we chapel people are much too good / for scoundrels like him. / He was one of eight, too, / each with a different surname ...' [Elfyn, 2012: 57]). The collection ends with a poem to her father on his death and the final verse is resonant with one of the most famous Welsh graces that children recite in school, proclaiming her thankfulness, having recognised in the earlier stanza that:

> Verses never leave me;
> daughter of the Manse,
> I had to learn the longest verse

> without understanding that the smallest
> is enough for a residue of prayer. (Elfyn, 2012: 125)

This is perhaps the clearest acknowledgement by Elfyn herself of the influence of religious discourse within her poetry. Her utilisation of liturgical and religious metaphors for the experience of voicelessness and the experience of speaking a stigmatised and sometimes subjugated language as a mother tongue helps us understand in greater depth the experience of bilingual women in Wales.

Elfyn: religion and women

Although her satirical poems are critical of religion's treatment of women, her sequence *Theology of Hair* (Elfyn, 1996: 57–69), which she regards as exemplifying her exploration of women's experience (Elfyn, 2010: 57), is more serious in tone. The sequence starts with exploring the experience of being in a chapel and seeing an array of female heads arousing in the poet a desire to touch and play with them. She suggests that this is not erotic but innocent (57), though a major theme in the sequence is to question why female hair is so threatening to patriarchal religion. For Elfyn, male sexuality and the desire to control women, particularly within a religious context, has led women to a lonely and alienating place (58).

In one poem in the sequence, *A God-Problem* (Elfyn, 2007: 53), Elfyn is more outspokenly critical and hair is referred to as symbolic of the violence which religion has inflicted on women:

> Standing before your altar,
> in my worst nightmares, I see
> a woman, shorn, being drowned as a witch,
> each single hair plucked out. (Elfyn, 2007: 55)

This dilemma leads the poet to question Jesus directly (Elfyn, 2010: 59):

> Jesus, what would you say today
> to women who wear veils?
> Is there a place for us in your sanctum? (Elfyn, 2007: 53)

The poem ends with a longing to hear the story of the woman who washed Jesus' feet, drying them with her hair, an action that no one, not even Jesus, stopped. However, the treatment of women by religion has caused the poet to have 'A God Problem' and in this Elfyn seems to align herself with a feminist or even post-feminist critique of Christianity (see for example Daly, 1986; Hampson, 1990). In *Hairdresser* (Elfyn, 2007: 57), there is a humorous treatment of gender difference, using biblical language and metaphor self-consciously in the rhythms and length of the lines (Elfyn, 2010: 60). An important facet of Elfyn's exploration of women's experience is that of motherhood, which also appears in this sequence.

Elfyn: motherhood

Elfyn is regarded as the first Welsh poet who has written honestly about the subject of miscarriage and her early volume *Stafelloedd Aros*[27] (1978) is considered to be radical and groundbreaking in this regard, as well as deeply moving (Marks, 2013: 87). Elfyn herself considers motherhood as an important theme within her work, as I have already mentioned, and explores it not only in terms of her own role but as a daughter too and in *Theology of Hair sequence IV Mother Tongue* (2007; 55, 57), relating it to language:

> The old language between mother and daughter.
>
> At times of sickness she'd be there,
> her palm flat on my forehead,
> chasing a curl away ... (2007: 55, 57)

This is not an idealised image, as the poet talks about how she would cringe when her mother did this when she was younger. Generally, her discussion of motherhood is one which turns the concept on its head, for example, she uses the mythical domestic voice of motherhood to condemn war (Marks, 2013: 98).

This is arguably one of the most characteristic voices and identity within her work (Marks, 2013: 87). Motherhood for her is infused with loss, joy and guilt (Elfyn, 2010: 10–14) and it is also a spur to pacifism, radicalisation and protest (Marks, 2013: 220). Her poetic exploration of this theme expresses the complexity and ambivalence of women's experience of motherhood and how it can become a potential gateway into a new form of empowerment, as also articulated by some of the women in my study.

Elfyn: summary

Elfyn's work shows a deep ambivalence towards religion; however, the influence of religious imagery and language on her work is evident. The themes that have emerged in my research conversations have also arisen in Elfyn's writing: the potential for empowerment in motherhood, voice and voicelessness, the resonance of social space (chapel and prison) and the repressive nature of traditional Welsh Christianity.

Despite her particular religious upbringing the poetic voice in Elfyn's work is a critical one and she notes the traditions and experiences which can lead to agency and flourishing, and critiques the dominant patriarchal discourses of church and chapel life with satire and humour. In Elfyn's work, the 'Ladies' no longer want to stay behind, but want to challenge crass and insensitive sermons, devise their own liturgies and sing their own psalms of protest.

Her work shows the possibility of a deep reflection on the themes of voice, religion, identity and women and how to satirise or even reimagine the oppressive context in which women find themselves. The traditional roles for women are overturned and the Welsh Mam of industrialisation has now become a protestor at Greenham Common. Her work is an example of how women today are playing an active part in their own identity construction; this shows the potential for a poetic theology to empower and inspire women through the use of difference genres including satire, creativity and imagination.

No Son Cristianos: *Mererid Hopwood*

Hopwood's role within the Welsh poetic tradition is also significant. In many ways she could be seen as the natural successor to Elfyn, given her political and language commitments (she is a member of the pacifist organisation Cymdeithas y Cymod). She is highly significant in the history of Welsh poetry as she was the first woman to win the Bardic Chair at the National Eisteddfod (2001). The chair is given to the best *awdl* (ode) poem and is the most prestigious of the awards. She has subsequently published an English-language book on the *cynghanedd* which is a distinctively Welsh form of strict metre used in Welsh poetic forms such as the *englyn* and *awdl*. Her winning poem was entitled *Dadeni* (Renaissance or rebirth) and describes the profound experience of losing a child leading to a renewal or rebirth, or even a sense of empowerment. It appears in *Nes Draw*, her only published collection of poetry (for adults).

In this collection, there is a similar engagement with religion as we find in Elfyn's work. In *No Son Cristianos*, there is harsh criticism of the missionary movement, colonialism and Western war and violence in the name of Christianity, and as the title suggests, a questioning of whether this is in fact following the teachings of Christ. Within Western colonialism, supposedly in the name of Christ:

> *Mae'r Gwynfydau'n goelcerth fwg.*
> The Beatitudes a smouldering bonfire. (Hopwood, 2015: 41, my translation)

God seems distant in her work, reminiscent of R. S. Thomas's fast God in *Pilgrimages*, who has left as soon as we have arrived. For example in *Paderau* (Prayers) God is absent, and this is also a theme in *Dadeni* – can the poet trust that God is present? There is a longing to believe here rather than feel anger towards God. In *Y Tymhorau* (Seasons) another priest poet, Euros Bowen, is echoed in her phrase *Bydd bywyd fyw byth* ('Life will live for ever' – my translation) (Hopwood, 2015: 99).

However her main influence is the poet Waldo Williams: she is an honorary president of the Waldo Williams society and has written an introduction to a reissue of a collection of his poems. Waldo Williams is well-known in Wales for his religious poetry, and a famous poem *Mewn Dau Gae* ('Between Two Fields', translated by Rowan Williams into English and available widely) speaks of his mystical experience of God in his native Llandysilio. Clearly Hopwood has been influenced by Williams's work and there are themes of loss and margins in her collection. *Nes Draw* means close–distant and several of the poems explore this theme of boundaries, parallels and paradoxes, as the title suggests. Hopwood's poetic voice is also therefore part of the tradition of religious poetry in Wales, especially in its connection to the landscape, though this is sometimes reimagined as the female divine (as in *Alaw*) as opposed to a straightforward sacramental and more traditionally Christian approach, as we get in Bowen.

The language and themes of scripture are implied in several of the poems, for example, Psalm 46 is reflected in *Cymorth Hawdd Ei Gael* ('A Very Present Help'). *Tua'r Dechreuad* is resonant with the rhythm of the Genesis creation story, and *Drws Gobaith*, a reflection on, as she puts it 'a place near St David's', is the story of the disciples meeting the resurrected Jesus on the Emmaus road:

> *Trwy wyrth y gair, torth a gwin,*
> *– Hen wledd pob gwir ryfeddod.*
> Through miracle of word, bread and wine,
> – ancient feast of every true wonder. (Hopwood, 2015: 63, my translation)

Jesus and God are addressed directly in some of her poems, and there is reference to sacrificial and Eucharistic imagery in her poem in memory of Helen Thomas (*Dim Cyffwrdd*) who died at Greenham Common. (Elfyn has also written about Greenham Common and Helen Thomas's death.)

Hopwood and Elfyn work within different traditions – Hopwood writes within strict metre, and Elfyn in *vers libre*, Hopwood is more within the poetic establishment of Wales perhaps. Hopwood's poetic voice is more connected to the landscape than people, unlike Elfyn. However, motherhood and loss and even disjuncture are key themes for Hopwood. In *Bore Oes*, the birth of a son is a moment of disconnection, as well as a moment of rebirth. Her poem *Fesul Un* ('One by One') asks Jesus to support those mothers who have lost children:

> *Clyw, Iesu, aros heno ar ddi-hun*
> *'da'r fam sy'n cyfri'r golled fesul un.*
> Listen, Jesus, stay awake tonight
> With the mother who counts her losses one by one. (Hopwood, 2015: 8, 7, my translation)

Although Hopwood and Elfyn are positioned differently within the Welsh poetic tradition, both speak into the figured world of my research participants where motherhood is an opportunity for empowerment, is not an idealised experience but one of loss and pain as well as growth. Hopwood's *Dadeni* ('Rebirth') is a clear example of this. It is a moving, delicate poem exploring the process of falling in love, the growth of new life within her body, the death of her child, and the search for God and meaning. There is also hope within this tragic experience – of pain bringing her to birth as a new person and looking towards the future.

The next conversation partners are women's voices in memoir, and in this next section I explore how three significant Welsh memoirs also engage with religion and identity.

Charlotte Williams: Sugar and Slate

Sugar and Slate (Williams, 2002) is a memoir which won the Arts Council of Wales Book of the Year 2003 award for its exploration of Williams's dual identity as Welsh–Guyanese. This memoir is a candid and qualitatively rich reflection on race, identity and belonging. For Williams, religion is an important part of her mother's identity, but not her own. To be a Welsh woman, as far as her portrait of her mother is concerned, is to be religious, resilient and assertive; again, the themes that emerged in my research conversations.

Charlotte Williams's engagement with identity is ambivalent: she expresses the confusion and alienation of being both mixed race and Welsh, and an English monoglot in a bilingual community. Although her white Welsh mother is seen sometimes as more of a stranger to British society than her Guyanese father, nevertheless her mother is agentic and strong, sustained by a keen biblical faith.

The book opens as Williams is reflecting on previous journeys to Africa, when her mother was forceful and confident when she was treated badly in a queue; this is a prelude for Williams to recall the comment made by her (African) father that 'because Ma was Welsh' she would not 'take orders from anybody' (Williams, 2002: 8). Williams reflects on a powerful sense of alienation throughout the book. She felt that she belonged neither in Wales nor in Guyana. This leads to an interesting discussion as to whether her black father or her white Welsh mother was the more estranged from English society. Surprisingly, she suggests that it is her mother:

> Dad was artist-in-residence at the Slade for a while. He became the interesting chap to have at parties; a curiosity, a poodle, the comfortable stranger. Ma was not so easy. She was Welsh and uncomfortably different. 'You're the English one,' she used to say to Dad, knowing in her heart that she was the real dark stranger. (10)

Williams also writes that her mother was religious in her own way and 'wielded Bible metaphor like a weapon' (11). To be Welsh according to Williams was to be religious:

> She was not a preacher like her sister Maggie, but her speech was framed with spiritual reference. I never remember her having any small talk; it wasn't her way. I think this is how we understood her as Welsh at first. Contrary, confrontational, biblical and a passionate stranger. (12)

Williams also describes her own alienation at an orientation meeting for those working overseas (her husband worked for the Overseas Development Administration) when she felt significantly and uncomfortably different from everyone else:

> Somehow the standard orientation package didn't fit the bill. Everybody else at Farnham, both staff and participants, were very white and very English and I suddenly felt very black and very Welsh. (103)

When she arrived in Guyana, the experience of being amongst other black people made her initially feel 'whole' again (105). This eventually became a confusing and ambivalent experience, because amongst the Guyanese she felt very British and although her father was originally Guyanese, as a north Walian, Africa did not feel like home for her either (121). She was never at ease with the 'expat' life and she explores the sense of hurt, shame and embarrassment resulting from others' casual racist assumptions. She felt responsible for her difference, silenced and forced into compliance (123).

Her reflections on missionary work in Africa, which form part of her writing about her Guyanese experience, were again informed by her Welsh identity. She considers that the church was a positive influence and that it played a contradictory role in both colonising and fighting against colonisation and slavery. It also provided hope and a means of fighting back for slaves. She writes that church was:

> ... one of the few ways in which they [slaves] could hold on to themselves as human beings. The Church provided the hope of equality and freedom for them, but more to the point, it provided the only legitimate place they could assemble ... It is a paradox that the Church pew was both the seat of the colonization of the slave mind and the seat of revolution. The very act of bringing the slaves together for worship gave them the opportunity to resist the plantocracy. (129)

Yet this chapel was also evocative for her of an older African tradition, as well as an ambivalent place of colonisation–revolution, calling to mind her father's discourse about the 'eternal presence of the ancestors' (131).

This duality of identity and the accompanying feeling of not really belonging anywhere was also an experience for Williams in Wales. As someone who did not speak Welsh fluently, this also made her feel alienated and even angry, and she describes, towards the end of the book, an argument she had with some Québécois whilst in Guyana:

> I could feel the anger welling. 'What about Wales where I live,' I threw in. 'You can't be Welsh unless you speak the bloody language. It's ridiculous ... now we're seen as outsiders in our own country because we can't speak Welsh.' I was angry with the politics of Wales. It felt like a double whammy – damned if you do and damned if you don't. There seemed to be no way to be Welsh unless it was apologising for not speaking Welsh, one of those Not-identities again ... Despite Ma, despite everything, I realised I didn't feel in any way claimed by Wales. (144)

Williams comments that because of the perception of Wales being the first colonised country, that she is aware of the feeling that 'the nigger man and the Welsh man are one' (Williams, 2002: 176), though race is still a complex issue in Wales, particularly in areas which are not racially diverse. Towards the end of the book she seems to be able to integrate all the different aspects to her identity and, on the birth of her granddaughter, begins to dream of the future for Wales and is at peace with her identity as a black Welsh woman:

> I know why it is that I like Wales. I like it because it is fragmented, because there is a loud bawling row raging, because its inner pain is coming to terms with difference and its divisions, because it realises it can't hold on to the myth of sameness, past or present ... (191)

Williams's book points to the role of religion as one part of what makes someone 'Welsh'– her mother's Welshness seems inextricably linked with that of the Bible and Christianity in general, and though Williams herself values the role of religion within the cultures of Wales (and Guyana), it does not seem to feature significantly in her own life. Ma's Welshness is described as an alien identity, though I wonder whether Williams is envious in that at least her mother's identity is more straightforward than her own. Her passion comes through her writing when she describes the sense of alienation from any culture or nationality, where she is not fully a member of any national group. Ma's Welsh identity is seen as more confident and strong than her own ambivalent search for belonging.

The tone of the memoir and the voice we hear in Williams's writing is angry, wistful, confused and searching. Her characterisation of her mother is certainly resonant of the trope of the Welsh Mam or Welsh Strong Woman. There is a contradiction here. Although Williams acknowledges the oppression, certainly in terms of language and a loss of language, that Welsh people have faced (144), she presents her mother as exhibiting a proud and effective resistance identity (Castells, 2010), one in which religion plays a significant part. However, religion is irrelevant to Williams, is part of her past but not of her present.

Jan Morris: Conundrum

My next memoir is by Jan Morris (2010), the well-known journalist and travel writer who was born in 1926 as a man. This book is illuminating in that Morris has insights into how British and Welsh cultures relate to men and to women differently and again, religion has, unexpectedly, been a main feature of Morris's upbringing, though it does not seem to be an important aspect of her life now.

As a child she had a strong sense of identity – she had not felt alienated, given that there was a strong sense within the family that they 'sprang ... from a line of odd forebears and unusual unions, Welsh, Norman, Quaker' and she comments that she 'never supposed myself to be much like anyone else' (Morris, 2010: 83–4). In fact her father was Welsh (her mother was English), and her father's relatives her cousin described as 'decent proud people' (90) conforming to stereo-typical Welsh characteristics such as having a love of music and writing, something she herself shared.

She describes an astonishing sense of acceptance at Oxford (where she went to boarding school) in that the culture there (as well as, incidentally, her Welsh back-ground) had no issue with the more 'feminine' pursuits:

> The school itself was sensible and un-hearty: nobody called me cissy for my poetic poses, or thought me silly when I blushed to expose my private parts. I detested sports, except cross-country running, but nobody held it against me and the more sensitive of the staff, I think, recognized some ambiguity in me and did their best to temper it. (220–3)

This acknowledgement of a more ambiguous sexual identity was also apparent in church and although Morris does not regard herself particularly as religious, it is clear that services gave her nourishment and space with which to explore her gender questions. In fact church (Christ Church Cathedral in Oxford) seems to be a place for Morris in which gender lines are blurred:

The noblest aspects of the liturgy aspired to what I conceived as the female principle. Our very vestments seemed intended to deny our manhood and the most beautiful of all the characters of the Christian story, I thought, far more perfect and mysterious than Christ himself, was the Virgin Mary, whose presence drifted so strangely and elegantly through the gospels, an enigma herself. (265–8)

She describes how the dualism of the Christian faith that was conveyed here allowed her to escape bodily preoccupations. Morris was able to distance herself from and therefore name and articulate an English identity which is usually considered 'norm' rather than 'other'. In her memoir she portrays Welsh artistic sensibilities and upper-class Englishness as a combination of cultures which allowed her to explore her growing sense of confusion about her gender identity and, in discussing sexuality in her early years, commented:

But the whole of English upper-class life, as I was later to discover more explicitly, was shot through with bisexual instinct. The public school system, the inhibitions of English manners, the happy tolerance accorded to originals and mavericks of every kind—all these traits meant that male relationships were full of emotional nuance and undertone. (435–8)

In this section of the memoir Morris appears to grow in her sense of alienation: her dual English–Welsh heritage, and her biological sex as male but desire to be female, lead her to feel estranged from others (510–11) and not even possessing an identity (533) – a version perhaps of the 'not-identity' as Williams discusses above.

Morris later describes her journey of changing biological sex, even living for a while in Oxford as a woman and elsewhere as a man. Finally, at home in Wales, she began to live as a woman, having to pretend that she and her wife were sisters-in-law, and before her operation she spent one last summer as a man in Llanystumdwy – a place she admits she felt she 'most truly belonged' (1592).

Morris's discussion of Welshness is interesting. She regards the Welsh gregariousness (*hwyl*) as part of an uncertainty and insecurity, a coping mechanism, then claiming that 'the Welsh love to show off their distinction, translating the national hwyl into perpetual performance'; similarly, her own emotionalism she regards as 'pure Welsh: so is the quick emotionalism, the hovering tear, the heart-on-sleeve, the touch of *schmaltz*, which has given my books the more sickly of their purple passages'. Interestingly she also regards her affinity to spirituality and an 'extrasensory streak' as springing 'directly from the strangeness of Wales' (1646–52). This she ascribes to the location and place of Wales as 'on the edge' (1656).

Yet, despite Morris having lived openly as a woman in Oxford, she chose to live first in Wales as a transgender woman, commenting that Welsh culture (that of Eifionydd in Gwynedd) was more accepting. I quote this excerpt at length because it is surprising and illuminating, contradicting a stereotype of Welsh people having traditional and conservative views of gender and sexuality:

Fortunately for me, the first society into which I ventured frankly and publicly sex-changed was the profoundly civilized society of Caernarfonshire. The Welsh are kind to most people and especially kind to their own. My neighbours and friends at Trefan, the villagers of Llanystumdwy, the farmers all around, the shopkeepers of Cricieth down the road, the community of artists, writers and philosophers who lived along the coast—all greeted my moment of metamorphosis with an urbane insouciance. It is a perturbing experience, to walk for the first time in skirts into a shop, say, whose people have known you for a male for many years and it was instructive to see how the Welsh coped with it. Some could not restrain a kind of gasp, instantly stifled. Some tactfully said how well I looked that morning. But most, with that accomplishment of performance which is the national birthright, simply pretended not to notice, spoke to me as they always did, asked after the children and by the skill of their pose put me at my ease and in their debt. (1825–32)

In terms of how she was treated as a woman, Morris argues that, despite feminism, men and women are treated differently. Women are not expected to be competent or independent and are patronised:

We are told that the social gap between the sexes is narrowing, but I can only report that having, in the second half of the 20th century, experienced life in both roles, there seems to me no aspect of existence, no moment of the day, no contact, no arrangement, no response, which is not different for men and for women. The very tone of voice in which I was now addressed, the very posture of the person next in the queue, the very feel in the air when I entered a room or sat at a restaurant table, constantly emphasized my change of status. (1841–5)

This experience is significant in that most of us never experience what it feels like to be a member of the other gender. Morris's experience as a transgender Welsh woman is unusual and her experience is very informative, as well as humorous:

I discovered that even now men prefer women to be less informed, less able, less talkative and certainly less self-centred than they are themselves: so I generally obliged them. (1852–3)

I expected to find in Morris's memoir discussion about gender and sexuality and about Welshness; however, I was surprised that there were so many references to religion (though admittedly not committed faith) and it seems that Morris's view of spirituality is based on an older, 'Celtic' spirituality rather than that more directly influenced by chapel culture. Morris comments that:

Images of magic have abounded in this book, wizards and wise women, miracles and virgin birth. I interpreted my journey from the start as a quest, sacramental or visionary and in retrospect it has assumed for me a quality of epic, its purpose unyielding, its conclusion inevitable. (2044–6)

The Welsh culture portrayed in this memoir is of acceptance and generosity where strangeness and the other is embraced. The gender and sexual confusion of her school days, in which religion played a significant part (though admittedly an English public-school religiosity), also enabled Morris to accept herself in her ambiguity. The Welsh identity she portrays is an attractive one, bounded to the land, creativity and the emotions. The religious tradition that has most affected

Morris is early Christian, or pre-Christian, with a sense of journey, quest and connection to the land and people.

Jasmine Donahaye: Losing Israel

Donahaye's *Losing Israel* won the Wales Book of the Year for Non-Fiction in the English Language Category in 2016 and is a remarkable book exploring Dona-haye's connection to Israel. Donahaye has lived and worked in Wales for several decades and has learnt Welsh and speaks it fluently. Donahaye is a secular Jew and the memoir explores the centrality of Jewishness for her identity and in particular the role of Israel within this.

Part travelogue, part memoir, the book is not a narrative account of her life but a deep reflection on the ambivalence of being a Jewish woman wanting to find belonging in Israel whilst struggling with the political situation there, and the displacement and ongoing oppression of Palestinians. During the course of the memoir we find out, to Donahaye's dismay, that her own family contributed to the displacement of a Palestinian community. However, even before this knowledge, her engagement with her parents' homeland is profound and unsettling.

One quotation, in Welsh, at the beginning of the book is from J. R. Jones (Donahaye, 2015: 6) describing his painful experience of feeling that you are not leaving your country, but that your country is 'leaving' you. She describes her own discomfort in this way:

> It is always a relief to leave, but always, as soon as I have left, the homesickness starts up, a longing to go back – this intense, contorted, alert consciousness, a kind of hyper-reality. (12)

This experience of not really belonging anywhere, of a permanent nostalgia/*hira-eth* is reminiscent of the experience of Stefania and her dual national identity of being Italian–Welsh. Like Charlotte Williams, Donahaye's relationship with Israel is linked to her relationship with her mother:

> Israel is inextricably caught up with my mother – my inaccessible, elusive mother, who left her community and her country, but inwardly never left, who carried her home, all the years of my childhood not in a book, as some anti-Zionists will say the 'true' Jew does, but in the locked chamber of her heart. (15)

Although raised on a kibbutz, Donahaye's grandmother separated from her grandfather and had an affair with a married man; as a result Donahaye's mother always felt 'part outsider' (16) after leaving with Donahaye's father to go to England, settling and raising Donahaye and her brother there. This was not a comfortable experience because of her mother's homesickness: 'Homesickness, and the longing for return, saturated my childhood. My mother's yearning was palpable' (19). This also made her mother inaccessible, and Donahaye always felt a sense of 'missing' her mother even when they were together:

> Even when I was with her, I missed her, because part of her was always missing – part of her was inaccessible, is still inaccessible, lost inside the cold, hard lock-up of her

soul, which the kibbutz exacted from every child as the cost of the ideal, new, egalitarian society. (20)

She describes how in the Hebrew language her mother becomes a different person, something which she finds she 'can't bear' as her mother becomes extroverted and lively in her own mother tongue (24). At ten years old Donahaye becomes fully aware of being detached from her mother, leading to a sense of isolation and loneliness for which she blames Israel (27). Yet, ironically, her mother is also alienated for leaving the kibbutz and Israel, considered 'the worst form of national treachery', something which 'lingered and festered like a curse' (31). Donahaye felt that she could put this right by herself returning to Israel as a young adult and the memoir describes the push–pull of Israel for her, as a longing to return in order to find not just herself but also her mother (41).

However, knowing that her own family had taken part in the displacement of Palestinians several decades ago, and knowledge of the current political situation in Israel/Palestine has led to her rejecting the romanticism and idealisation of her past. Donahaye asks:

> … who can ever be fully at home in the world when the home rests on the homelessness of others? I could not be at home there – but I wonder if I can ever fully be at home anywhere else. (42)

She then describes how she took refuge in California where she could revel in an uncomplicated Jewish identity, then conducted her own PhD research in Wales where she explored Wales's past use of Israel as a model for its own sense of nationhood: 'Moving to Wales and engaging with its troubles was a form of Zionism displaced, a love of Wales-as-Israel' (44).

The reality of the displacement of Palestinians, and the fact that she has been encouraged to develop her personal identity in opposition to an Arab 'other', feels uncomfortable and shameful (70). She finds herself fetishising Arab men, and in describing her attraction to 'Abu Omar's grandson' whom she has met in the course of her research, and then other Arab men, she has a sexually confident tone, which is qualitatively different from the tone of the women in this study:

> The ache of desire is sehnsucht, hiraeth, saudade – a tearing loneliness of the soul, a longing to come home. Instead of carrying my homeland in a book, in my heart, it has transferred to beautiful men with luminous dark eyes – 'the enemy', 'the other', since I can no longer love my own … I know I am committing in my fevered imagination every sin of exotification and objectification, of orientalism and sexual imperialism. (80)

Donahaye expresses liberal discomfort here rather than guilt associated with religion, and although she has adopted a Welsh identity and commitment, there is nothing in her experience of that chapel repressed sexuality that has been the backdrop to the lives of the women in my study, nor the other writers I discuss in this chapter. The shame that is central for Donahaye is not one based on feeling 'not good enough' but a dismay with what those sharing her social identity have done to others: 'I know where my family is from, but now I am ashamed of that place, ashamed of the crime and the destruction on which it was built' (133).

Although Donahaye admits she will never fully feel whole or at home anywhere, somehow she finds some peace and an imperfect sense of belonging in a Wales which has, at times, identified with an (albeit oppressed and isolated) Israel, with its Israeli-sounding chapel place names. She recognises that love is not diminished because the person or the place is 'stained' (194). She is resigned to her sense of ambivalent belonging.

Welsh women's literary voices

In this chapter I have explored the writings of two poets and three memoir writers in order to explore more deeply issues of identity and religion for Welsh women. This is in order to gain a wider and richer understanding, given that within qualitative research it is recognised that examining particular stories can help illuminate the general (see Plaskow and Christ, 1989: 5; Swinton and Mowat, 2006: 43; Wengraf, 2000: 161). In practical and feminist theology it is also recognised that literature is where women have done theology, particularly when more traditional and academic avenues have been closed to them. Within feminist theology, literature is where women have had space to explore difficult, complex and previously silenced experiences (Walton, 2007: 36).

The three memoirs contribute to the conversation with the research participants in different ways. Belonging and alienation are key themes in all three but particularly for Williams and Donahaye. Unexpectedly, the role of the mother has also been significant, and the salience of the trope of the Strong Woman/Welsh Mam was particularly strong in Williams's writing, but Donahaye also revealed a robust connection between national identity and her mother, even if she is speaking out of a different context and background. For her, there was less of a sense of a dominant mother, and more of an exploration of a flawed connection. The chapel culture which is permanently in the background of the other women I have spoken to or discussed is absent in her work, and, as a result, her writing about sexuality seems markedly different, less guilt-ridden, more agentic. Though for Morris, the generous acceptance of her transition from male to female also challenges the stereotype of Welsh morality as repressed and closed.

The Strong Woman stereotype was particularly evident in Williams's description of her mother, although Williams articulated a much more ambivalent, and even negative, sense of agency and confidence. For her the role of religion within Welsh identity is varied and ambivalent, empowering and disempowering – a religion which has the potential both to colonise and revolutionise.

Both Elfyn and Hopwood engage with Christianity critically and confidently in their poetry. For Hopwood, spirituality can be found in connectedness to landscape. God is both absent and everywhere, but Hopwood's relationship with the divine is not unquestioning and she is comfortable with ambiguity and paradoxes as the title of her collection shows. Elfyn's satire takes this a step further and offers a creative and empowering approach for women (and men) who want to engage with religion and faith on their own terms and challenge and laugh at what is unhelpful. Elfyn's fantasising about chanting a psalm telling Jesus to make his own cup of tea shows that the Welsh female poetic tradition also has resources to challenge injustice within the church. This demonstrates the potential of a feminist and poetic theological approach in naming oppressive practices and imagining a different future as important steps in bringing about change (Walton, 2014: 139).

7

In Conversation with the Strong Woman

This study has found that religion has been a formative influence for women who are currently middle-aged (and older). A significant feature of this influence has been an attempted socialisation into respectability by their families, characterised as 'the fear of what Mrs Jones down the road might say'. However middle-aged women are not instilling the same model of respectability into the lives of the next generation, and my research participants reported that institutional religion in particular was tangential to their lives. The influence of religion within Welsh women's identity is diminishing, and how Welsh identity is constructed is therefore in a state of flux.

Another important finding is that many Welsh women have an operative and empowering stereotype, the Strong Woman, and the women whom I interviewed or whose work I read did not simply talk about their high sense of agency but demonstrated it in their life stories. This contradicted my initial assumption that Welsh women lacked confidence and had low self-esteem.

In this chapter I bring the trope of the Strong Woman into conversation with other themes and writings. What challenge does the Strong Woman bring to our thinking about Welsh women's identity today?

Reinterpreting the Welsh Mam

The trope of the Welsh Strong Woman was created against a genteel moralistic identity of the English woman. Aaron maintains that nineteenth-century writing played a part in constructing a different kind of strength in morality for Welsh women, and points to Mary Oliver Jones's *Pur fel y Dur* as a story which contributed to the idiomatic saying that English women were like velvet but Welsh women were as pure as (and presumably as strong as) steel (Aaron, 1998: 8, 9). Various female postcolonial identities were similarly contrasted, that of the strong hardworking black woman or Indian woman with the weaker, white or English 'angel in the home' (ap Gareth, 2009: 88), stereotypes which were unhelpful for both postcolonial and English women, linked to class and respectability.

For my research participants the Strong Woman archetype was closely linked to that of the Welsh Mam. However the Strong Woman is a far more empowering trope for Welsh women than one which is linked to responsibilities for home and family. The combination of the Welsh Mam ideal and the women portrayed in advertising and in childcare manuals in the twentieth century put a distinctive pressure on Welsh women to become perfect wives and mothers (Beddoe, 2000: 138). For working-class women, there is still pressure to do the double shift of unpaid work in the home as well as their paid employment. Mannay refers to the '*ideology* of the Welsh Mam' (my emphasis, Mannay, 2016: 66) and argues on the basis of her own research that 'the domestic sphere remains a site of inequality' for working-class women (Mannay, 2016: 65).

Working-class women are evolving a new respectability based on juggling paid work, motherhood and performing the impossible expectations of being a 'domestic goddess' (Mannay, 2016: 82). This affects both feelings about the self and about their acceptability within society. Mannay reports that one of her participants, Bethan, found housework to be a 'psychological defence' against the stigma of being thought of as an inadequate mother (Mannay, 2016: 80). Another woman in her project referred to herself as a 'lazy bitch' because she and her partner shared domestic chores as they both worked full-time (Mannay, 2016: 81).

My own participants spoke about housework as a shared activity within marriage/heterosexual relationships, though this could be because they were mainly middle-class, and not having to earn their respectability in the same way as Mannay's participants. For example, Marged's family spoke about 'Dad's hoover'. Potential differences in class as indicated in the differences in response by my participants and Mannay's would be very useful to research further.

Another important aspect of the Welsh Mam as a problematic archetype for Welsh women is that it does not adequately represent the experiences of all women – for example gay women, or those who are not mothers (Rees, 2014: 348). For women who would have wanted to have children but were unable to for whatever reason, the stereotype is particularly painful. There are therefore dangers in overemphasising the Mam aspect of this archetype, and a way forward would be to develop the trope of the Strong Woman in order to supersede the Welsh Mam as a more helpful and inspiring stereotype for women.

In a recent Welsh newspaper the Welsh Mam is described in this way:

> There's a facial expression unique to Welsh mothers, affectionately known as 'Mamface', that could break up an LA gang fight. Deployed judiciously, it warns of extreme displeasure, rapidly diminishing tolerance and impending, possibly fatal, action. Welsh Mam holds no truck with negotiation or bribery. Do as she asks or die. Just as formidable is Welsh Nain, a matriarchal grandmother who invariably 'could have gone out with Tom Jones' and aggressively feeds all visitors like *foie gras* geese. 'C'mon, just a small snack is all', Welsh Nain will say at 11pm, as she bungs in a leg of lamb and pops on the bakestone to make three dozen Welshcakes. Resistance is futile.[28]

In this humorous excerpt, hospitality is seen as important for the Welsh Mam but what is striking is her fearsomeness – this particular paragraph in the newspaper was titled 'There is nothing more terrifying than a Welsh mam'. The advantage of focusing on the Strong Woman as an empowering stereotype is that it redirects expectations of women away from the Welsh Mam's domestic role and towards empowerment.

One portrayal of a Welsh Mam which has had influence on Welsh tropes is the mother in *How Green Was My Valley* (Llewellyn, 2011), written in 1939, with the film version released in 1941. In the book, the mother is characterised as resilient and is open-minded and critical of how those in the chapel treat a woman who is cast out of chapel for falling pregnant out of wedlock. In the Oscar-winning film version, the character, played by Dublin born Sara Allgood,[29] threatens to kill anyone who continues to criticise her husband for not supporting their strike. Although this is costly for her, despite putting on a show of bravery in front of the men, on the way back in the cold night she falls into the river and has to be saved by her son Huw. He then, as a result, becomes very ill for a period of time. However, the show of strength in her speech is remarkable:

> I have come up here to tell you what I think of you all, because you are talking against my husband. You are a lot of cowards to go against him. He has done nothing against you and he never has and you know it well. How some of you, you smug-faced hypocrites, can sit in the same chapel with him I cannot tell. To say he is with the owners is not only nonsense but downright wickedness. There's one thing more I've got to say and it is this. If harm comes to my Gwilym, I will find out the men and I will kill them with my two hands. And this I will swear by God Almighty.[30]

Again, this iconic representation of the Welsh Mam has strength at its core, and resonates with the experience of the women in my research conversations who valued strength as well as family, connection and community. An overemphasis on the Welsh Mam can lead to an over-identification of women with motherhood and a domestic role. However, it can also help us value the wisdom and contribution of older women and reinforce the importance of community and networks. By emphasising the Strong Woman and utilising the Welsh Mam's strength and wisdom we can develop an inclusive trope for women and encourage women as individuals to be agentic within their own lives, and fulfil their potential freed from roles and others' expectations.

A new dissent: embodied, embracing, poetic

An important aspect of the Strong Woman is her empowerment, and this trope speaks directly into an important Welsh Christian tradition of dissent. Standing up to religious power and calling it to account is an important part of the Welsh theological tradition, as was seen in the move for disestablishment. This political movement to separate the Church in Wales from the Church of England and remove some of the Anglican Church's financial and political privileges and powers was resisted by Anglicans in Wales, but was supported by the Free Churches in part because of the animosity created by having predominantly English-speaking bishops and clergy, and the way in which the Free Churches were treated unfavourably in comparison with the numerically weaker Church of England in Wales (Walker, 1976: 160–7). However, it also reveals a strand within the Welsh Christian tradition which is resistant to a state church and challenges power whether it is located in individuals or organisations.

This study has shown that there is a longer tradition of dissent within Wales which is about transgressing the moral codes others have designed. This is shown in the provocative poetry of Gwerful Mechain and her praise poem to the vagina, as well as her other poems which challenge the poetic establishment of the day. The postcolonial feminist theologian Althaus-Reid writes about the importance of an 'indecent theology' in words which could be easily applied to Gwerful Mechain's poetry and what it can inspire in Welsh women today as a new form of dissension:

> One cannot submit to sexual decency master codes without tacitly submitting to politi-
> cal master codes too. Decent Christian women unfortunately, make decent citizens too.
> However, it is from indecent Christians and subversive citizens that action for transfor-
> mation occurs in history. Indecency may be the last chance for a surplus of Christianity
> to transform political structures. (Althaus-Reid, 2000: 170)

Mechain's work shows that there are even theological traditions within Wales which can be used to challenge the repressed and respectable identities created for Welsh women, which they now find unhelpful and even oppressive. It is important to promote an appreciation of the role of dissent within the Welsh tradition, not as another form of social control, but as a way of encouraging individuals and groups to feel themselves empowered and able to critique those who hold power, both political and social.

In developing a new dissent we could also point to Volf's (1996) theology of embrace as encouragement to utilise what is useful within all the theological traditions of Wales rather than ignore or characterise them as 'other'. If, in Wales, we have constructed religious identities based on difference rather than similarity, as seen in the church/chapel divide, now is the time to set them aside. One of the treasures of Welsh Nonconformity is a radical commitment to equality, and ironically, an embodied, visceral and poetic faith which has inspired the hymns for which Wales is so famous. We have an opportunity to challenge the stereotype of 'chapel' being dry and dualistic in its approach to body and spirituality. In fact this comment by Gwyn Jones suggests that even though chapel buildings are designed for a cerebral and narrowly spiritual engagement with God, Welsh people have turned them into a sensuous experience:

> ...today their power weakens, but for three Welshmen [*sic*] out of four the gleam of the
> varnished pew, the smell of the polished linoleum, the ecstatic rustle of a rising congre-
> gation, and maybe the taste of a hymn-book cover, are unforgettably part of those child-
> hood years when in sensuous innocence we stood a rung nearer heaven. (Jones, 1948:
> 24; in Bruce, 2010)

The Welsh poetic tradition is one place where dissent and embodiment are held together, and the present moment as sacrament pervades the work of Nonconformist, Anglican and Catholic poets alike.

A poetic approach

If theology has always been found in hymnody, poetry and, non-verbally, in ritual (Bevans, 2009: 17) then we can look to poetry and hymns to discern the theological commitments within Welsh identity. Poetry, Allchin argues, is a much less rarefied pursuit in Welsh-speaking communities than in the English-speaking world as it is a commonplace interest for people in every walk of life. Because of the pervasiveness of poetry, people are both 'priests' and 'poets' because of the recognition of the glory in everyday activities, for instance, in celebrating your team's winning goal, a delicious meal, the applause at the end of a concert:

> ... all these acts of praise are acts which recognize, celebrate and proclaim some tiny revelation of the rightness of things. We have some awareness of wholeness, a glimpse of God's glory. (Allchin, 1991: 6)

The priest and poet are both called to bless, which Allchin regards in the original meaning as to 'speak good things' (6). However, the glory and praise are not seen in entirely positive terms. He refers to the complexity of this experience and articulation within the tradition which involves moral ambiguity and satire as well as religion and faith (20) and where prayer is seen as a 'kind of death' (161).

Allchin seems to be suggesting that the Welsh poetic tradition is more embodied, contextualised and multivalent than its English-speaking counterpart. In fact, in Welsh poetics, daily life is sanctified, as Gwenallt's poem about St David (in translation by Allchin) shows. The poem starts by saying that:

> There is no barrier between two worlds in the Church.
> The Church militant on earth
> Is one with the Church triumphant in heaven ...

Despite the vision Gwenallt describes of a unified heaven and earth, the image is very homely: St David accompanying schoolchildren and students, as a miner and factory worker, and, in this excerpt, as a housewife, bringing out the Eucharist like a family meal:

> He carried the Church everywhere
> Like a body with life and mind and will,
> And he did small things and great.
> He brought the Church into our homes,
> Put the holy vessels on the kitchen table
> With bread from the pantry and wine from the cellar,
> And he stood behind the table like a tramp
> So as not to hide from us the wonder of the sacrifice.
> (Gwenallt in translation, Allchin, 1991: 61)

In this tradition, boundaries between the secular and sacred, church and home, the domestic and public spheres are transgressed. This is also a feature of the Welsh female poetic tradition. I have already mentioned Gwerful Mechain and her praise poem to the vagina. Another significant Welsh female poet is the eighteenth-century hymn writer Ann Griffiths. She is better known than Mechain, and Allchin argues that she has a central place in British religious, and particularly literary, history (75).

What was exceptional about Ann Griffiths was her incarnational theological emphasis, focus on praise, the sacredness of everyday experience and the holiness of place, as well as the spiritually and affectively intense relationship with the divine she explores through poetry (71–105). In Ann Griffiths's work we also see the continuation of a tradition of the embodied and passionate faith we saw in Gwerful Mechain. Her articulation of desire directed towards Jesus Christ is astonishing given her rural eighteenth-century context. Her most famous hymn, *Lo Amid the Myrtles Standing* often sung to the tune *Cwm Rhondda*, says this about Christ:

> He is called the Rose of Sharon, / white and radiant, fair of face: / he excelleth o'er ten thousand / princes of our mortal race. (Ann Griffiths, translated by Jane Owen, Pwyllgor y Llyfr Emynau Cydenwadol, 2001: 302)

In the Welsh religious poetic tradition it could be argued that praise, the mystery of God and the ordinariness or even the negativity within daily life all combine in a tradition of 'Glory'. Despite this more complex and multi-layered understanding, Allchin argues that the tradition of praise within the Welsh poetic tradition is affirming of not just God but of humans, who are a sign of his creation:

> To praise another human being or any part of God's creation means to recognize, to celebrate and to proclaim the goodness which is in them. All goodness comes from God and is a sign of his presence in the world he has made (Allchin, 1991: 6).

The embodied, joyful and mystical tradition of Welsh religious poetry, where God is experienced powerfully in ordinary life, is a useful corrective to the repressive and oppressive stereotype of chapel culture. As an egalitarian activity, poetry within the Welsh tradition is also helpful to utilise within a new approach to religious dissension. This is one aspect of Christian practice in which the Free Churches have much to teach the Church in Wales.

Clericalism, mission and power

In 2012, the Church in Wales undertook a review, at the instigation of the Governing Body of the Church in Wales, because of an overwhelming perception, according to the report, of the need and commitment for 'change' (Church in Wales, 2012: 2). Although it was found that members were enthusiastic for change, this was not reflected in actual practice because of 'cultural and structural reasons' (3). The report identified 'a culture of deference and dependence' (4) and discussed practices in which clergy at a local level and bishops at a diocesan level were expected to be involved in minor decisions and take all the initiative resulting in a disempowered and frustrated laity (4). It noted an unhealthy deference to those in power and that ordinary members of the Church in Wales lacked a voice in its governance (4).

Although the review suggested practical ways of encouraging more lay participation in decision-making within the structures, the more worrying aspect of its comments was the culture it had identified. Given the prevalence of the trope of the Strong Woman within my findings it is surprising that the culture of the Church in Wales (at least) has been characterised by obsequiousness, apathy and disempowerment.

It is possible that the Strong Woman has not managed to find a place nor a voice within the Church in Wales and has simply left (it was only in 2013 that the episcopate was opened up to women in the Church in Wales, for example, and women were only allowed to be ordained priests in 1997). My research participants revealed that issues of justice were important to them: if they spoke about this in the interview they were highly critical of the inequalities between men and women in the church or spoke approvingly of women being ordained. Feminist theologians such as Graham (2009, Chapters 1–4) would argue that sexism and clericalism are closely linked. Therefore, it is vital if the Church in Wales wants to engage with middle-aged and younger women that it addresses both sexism and deference, learning from the Welsh Nonconformist tradition about the importance of equality and dissent. A distinctive and attractive feature of the Strong Woman's approach to dissent, however, is humour.

Humour as a dissenting discourse

A significant feature of the way both my research participants and the writers I studied resisted oppressive forces in their lives was through humour. Elfyn utilises satire effectively in her poetry to challenge religious stereotypes of Welsh women and the way they are treated in chapel life. Similarly the response of my research participants to attempts by others to coerce or control was to laugh at them.

Laughter is empowering for those with little power and is intimidating for the powerful (Bussie, 2007). Bussie suggests this is a particularly female contribution within theology, as laughter is neglected in white, male dominated Western theology (Bussie, 2007: 3), and she proposes an attention to a 'laughter from below' which can enrich and deepen our understanding of what it means to be human. A theology of laughter can help us to live more hopefully and reject dichotomies by holding experience and hope in tension, by dissenting from and subverting the dominant discourses and by being honest about the reality of suffering (183–93).

The humorous tone of several of my interviews reflected Bussie's argument about the hopefulness and subversion derived from humour. None of the women I spoke to said that they had experienced physical violence, though Hannah's marriage was an emotionally abusive one and several of the other participants had experienced psychological abuse and attempts by others to control them. It could be argued that it is easier to see humour in situations when our lives are reasonably safe and secure. However, this dissenting satirical approach to misogyny and sexism has been a way in which the participants have withstood suffering in the past and maintain their resilience. In my experience, many women have found strength and comfort in Elfyn's *Will the Ladies Please Stay Behind* and it is important for us to value and recognise the power of laughter to empower and heal. Humour is an important tool, and it also directly challenges stereotypes of Welsh religion as dry and dreary.

The African-American Matriarch and the Strong Woman

Although the silent woman identified by Western and, predominantly white, feminist theologians did not find resonance with the Welsh Strong Woman, there is a similarity with the trope of the African-American Matriarch. She is also 'strong, persevering and determined' (Snorton, 1996: 50) because she has learnt 'through experience that strength is a requirement, not a luxury, in her life' (54). Snorton argues that the qualitatively different experience of African-American women has been ignored in American feminist theology in favour of the passive victim trope beloved of white Western feminists (50). Although some of the related stereotypes are negative (she is also, for example, considered sexually aggressive, castrating and disempowering of men) (52) there are clear similarities between this trope and that of the Welsh Strong Woman, as well as common pastoral implications.

Snorton argues that the African-American Matriarch stereotype means that black women feel pressure to be strong for others, not to show vulnerability, and have learnt to cope by expecting the 'worst' to happen (50–65). This is a challenge for pastors in order to contribute to the right climate for the flourishing of these women and their communities, in working for the eradication of poverty and racism and genuinely working for opportunities for growth in all areas of life (62, 63).

Her work also points to the value placed within the African-American tradition of the self as placed not only in community (and that being a community within the present), but also within a cultural framework which values history and belonging:

> To be an African-American individually is interwoven with the collective generations of women of our same culture, both the 'ancients' and the 'bloodmothers, othermothers and women centred networks' of our own community ... (Snorton, 1996: 55)

She also notes the 'adaptive training' that mothers give daughters in how to survive physical and emotional oppression, in resilience, the ability to accept and overcome obstacles and, in particular, the utilisation of spirituality and selflessness (Snorton, 1996: 57–9). In fact relationships are vital for the African-American woman and she might not be able to identify with that longing to be a separate 'I' that is expressed within white Western feminist theology (Snorton, 1996: 63). This can help us understand the importance placed by the women in my study on the mother–daughter relationship and especially the significance the women placed on their mothers as their inspiration, even when they were critical of how they had socialised them into acceptance of a more subservient role within marriage and society.

Welsh women also find themselves more connected to others within their communities both past and present and find meaning in relationships of caring, experiencing them as life-giving rather than restricting. Perhaps, as in the case of the African-American Matriarch, the Welsh Mam has become an important stereotype within Wales in asserting and encouraging resilience and strength as part of a resistance identity in order to overcome oppression and stigmatisation.

101

Walton (2007) points to womanist theology as having a literary origin and argues that womanists 'were not defining themselves on the basis of the oppression they had suffered at the hands of whites but rather in relation to the creative genius of their own people' (Walton, 2007: 8). *The Color Purple* by Alice Walker is, of course, a key womanist text, highly influential within feminist theology (Walton, 2007: 11), and has also influenced women in Wales – see for example Helen Mary Jones's personal account of how the novel inspired her (Jones, 2010).

We also have a long and significant literary tradition which may also contribute to a more distinctive and robust identity. It is significant that a more positive and resilient social identity is present in cultural identities which value literary and creative traditions.

In this chapter I have argued that the Strong Woman trope is a more empowering and inclusive role model for women in Wales than the Welsh Mam. We have seen that although the mainly middle-class women in this research shared chores within their relationships, according to Mannay (2016) working-class women still feel pressure to be perfect wives and mothers in order for their own self-esteem and to gain respectability. This indicates a further avenue for exploration.

Other aspects of the Strong Woman trope useful for positive and empowering identities for Welsh women are her embodiment, dissent and humour as well as strength. As we notice that Welsh identities are in a state of flux, we have an opportunity to utilise what is positive about our religious traditions, especially dissent and a poetic faith. There is also scope to make connections between this trope and that of the African American Matriarch.

DAUGHTERS OF GWERFUL MECHAIN

Isn't everyone's relationship with God like that?
I wanted to ask, while our teacher
told us Ann Griffiths was a *mystic*.
At seventeen, boys are all-consuming,
even God. Now she lines the cold path
to Llanfihangel church. Blue Books

betrayed her legacy, leaving us heavy
gold edged Bibles, green gloss paint,
strict metre four part harmonies,
(unless your tenor has died,
or your alto babysitting grandchildren).
Our rooms – front parlours, sagging

with respectability. Ceramic angels,
genteel ladies, china cups gleaming
like women's sacrificed souls
on Wales's mantelpiece altar.
Ann, join with us and all
the daughters of Gwerful Mechain.

Let us dig up her work, plunder
our birthright, cast off
Victoriana felt and brass that stops us
breathe. Hunger for a passionate
God. Adore our bodies.
Relish the world. (Parry, 2009: 32)

8

Constructing New Identities

My research question was about the impact and importance of religion in the identities of Welsh women. It was raised initially by my own experience, and that of other women in the Church, of struggling with confidence and agency. I found that these discussions were also reflected within feminist pastoral theology and discussions about the self and women's role in the Church and society. Bennett Moore wrote:

> I have fought for self-confidence as a woman in the face of the kind of role, status and character for women projected by my father and my early Christian teaching, which made men the gateway to the real world ... In my pastoral work I have been astonished to discover many women with problems of self-confidence greatly in excess of my own. (Bennett Moore, 2002: 134)

Although the women I interviewed reported instances of discrimination and shaming practices, they also told stories of resilience and hope. Their discourse of strength was particularly impressive and inspiring, and, by reproducing their stories, my hope is that this will further encourage women in Wales to construct new and empowering identities for themselves. Is it, however, possible to reimagine and reinterpret religious practices and teaching in order to join in with this project?

As I have argued, it is possible to find resources within the Christian tradition to develop new theologies of personal identity which can lead to human flourishing rather than shaming or passivity. Similarly, there is also a task ahead to promote positive social identities for Welsh women not based on control and obedience, but which enable confidence and participation in community and national life rather than silence and submission.

If a new resistance identity was constructed for Welsh women as a response to the Blue Books' report, through the publication of *Y Gymraes* magazine, and strong church discipline exercised against women who became pregnant out of wedlock for the nineteenth and twentieth centuries, it must also be possible to construct positive identities in order to empower Welsh women (and men) for the twenty-first century. In this chapter I outline the remaining issues raised from this study that need addressing and offer suggestions for theology and the Church.

Addressing Shame

It is possible to interpret this study as a narrative of the use of shaming individuals and groups in order to exercise social order and control. Pattison, whose work I have used as a framework for this study, describes shame as a family of concepts including a fear of exposure, a feeling of not being good enough, of despair and isolation and a powerlessness and passivity (Pattison 2000: 74). It involves a sense of inferiority, personal diminishment (76) as well as defilement (90). Pattison critiques the Western Christian tradition for conflating guilt and shame, for not being specific enough about what constitutes sin, leading people to feel bad about who they are rather than what they may have done.

This has led to a situation where groups have been rejected, condemned and shamed for their social identities such as female gender or homosexuality (266). This emphasis on stigmatised identities rather than on damaging behaviours has skewed our understanding of what 'sin' actually is. Pattison points to the dynamics of shame around homosexuality where appearances and preservation of face and honour is seen as more important than being truthful, and a tacit acceptance of a 'don't ask, don't tell' policy (269). Discussions within the Church of England, and the focus on sexuality to the detriment of other topics, seem to suggest that who we are is far more problematic than what we do. Money, power and violence have the potential to be far more damaging to people's lives. However, sin is seen as being attached to the social identity of some rather than the moral behaviour of all.

Pattison notices that the use and abuse of shaming within Christianity has been a deliberate act of social control (270). He is also critical of the damaging effects of teachings about humility, particularly to those who are already feeling ashamed of who they are. This can lead to further passivity, self-obsession and depression and even 'hatred, self-righteousness and rigidity' (251). Again, this is not the sphere of love, acceptance, change and forgiveness but a form of Christianity which leads to a spiral of negativity rather than the life-giving possibilities of reconciliation and freedom from the past.

My own research participants would recognise this shaming as part of their background and upbringing and as something they entirely reject. Reflecting on the recent religious history of Wales, it is possible to interpret events since the Blue Books' report as the shamed Free Church leaders then, in turn, shaming Welsh women for supposedly immoral behaviour, and using the fear of exposure and rejection in order to exercise sexual and moral control over women's lives. As Pattison himself suggests, the Church is not unique in 'creating and exploiting shame', as it can be a feature of any social organisation (276). However, it is a particularly potent tool of the Church, which still has potential even now to be used to control members and maintain hierarchical power.

He suggests ways of addressing this, such as to be less idealistic and more practical in assessing the impact of Church teaching and practices, to change some pastoral and liturgical practices which encourage individuals to remain in a state of shame and alienation, and, finally, to critically assess and change symbols and theological ideas which also perpetuate shame in order to help 'realise the vision of human beings fully alive, communicating and communicant in a community of responsibility' (276). The goal is therefore flourishing individuals and communities who know and feel themselves to be empowered and agentic. There is a call here for churches to be more accepting of difference, to emphasise God's love and forgiveness in liturgy rather than sin, and above all to be places where human beings can be open and honest about their frailty and struggles rather than hide them.

The Western Christian tradition could be critiqued for not embedding a doctrine of the importance of human flourishing enough within its teachings, leading to a situation where all are made in the image of God but some are made in the image of God more than others. This has led to the situation where groups have been scapegoated, excluded and shamed, as has happened for Welsh women. Pattison's work also demonstrates the link between social and personal identity, where our membership of a particular social group can lead to individual negative emotions and sense of self, and the dangers of this for mental and emotional well-being.

Natals not mortals

One resource to promote a more positive dynamic for identity derived from the Christian tradition is in the work of Jantzen (1998) who encourages us to see human beings not as mortals but as natals. For Jantzen, mortality speaks of domination, control and death, what she calls the 'traditional theology of Christendom' (Jantzen, 1998: 157). She critiques Western Christianity with its emphasis on the cross and sin and practices such as hierarchies and tightly controlled membership, order, authority and exclusivity. Natality, on the other hand, emphasises justice and human flourishing (along the lines that I have already explored as a particular concern for Practical Theology in the introduction), and Jantzen suggests that it is a more positive metaphor than that of salvation which is 'embedded in an imaginary of death' (159).

Jantzen argues that natality encourages us to see humans as those who are born and continually living with the possibility of new birth and flourishing. She points to the biblical metaphor of needing to be 'born again' (as seen in the gospel according to John 3) in order to understand Christ's message about the Kingdom of God (143), as well as the biblical metaphor of flourishing and abundant life, as seen in Jesus' parables about seeds, growth, gardening and vines (158). She regards natality as a particularly fruitful concept for a renewed understanding of the Christian message and for shifting the practice and experience of Christianity from metaphors and language to do with death, control and authority to that of life, flourishing and growth. It is concerned with physical and psychological realities and well-being, whereas a faith built on salvation can often be too focused on spiritual experience or life after death (167).

If Christian institutions in Wales taught and practised the importance of personal creativity, growth and empowerment, individuals and communities would be transformed. As Jantzen has shown, there are resources within the Christian tradition and, in particular, in the teachings of Christ for flourishing to be the dominant metaphor for the role of the church, communities and individuals. However, as we have seen, the recent history of the church shows that it has sought to control and shame rather than encourage individuals and communities to grow and thrive. A significant aspect of controlling and shaming is also to do with class, another important finding derived from this research.

Class and respectability: the monster we have created

A significant aspect of Welsh identity is a self-perception of egalitarianism (Trosset, 1993). A perception of Wales's 'classlessness' possibly originates from the rural experience where people of different social and economic status lived in the same community. Although there are large differences in income, they are not as marked as in other parts of the UK and social stratification can be along other lines, for example, respectability (Evans, 2010: 131) or as previously discussed, 'Welshness' (Trosset, 1993). Whilst I acknowledge that attitudes to class and stratification are something which makes Wales distinctive from other parts of the UK (Evans, 2010: 154), my findings were that class is a surprisingly significant concept within Welsh female identity. My participants revealed tension and unhappiness with the way Welsh society is stratified and felt that poverty did lead to a sense of shame and unworthiness, more so than the 'classless' myth of Wales would suggest.

My participants critiqued the lack of acknowledgement of issues of class and power within public life as hypocritical, and pointed to a disjuncture between perception and reality. Jessie, for example, pointed to the Welsh middle-class elite as utilising a 'chapel' identity as well as language and other 'Welsh' pursuits and practices whilst (in some cases purposefully) alienating the working classes. She was particularly scathing of their tactics of excluding others through language, or deliberately using grammatically correct and opaque language in order to confuse ordinary Welsh speakers. There was also a perception that this group looks down on the working class whilst romanticising it and even appropriating this identity for themselves, hanging paintings of miners or quarrymen in their expensively furnished houses whilst talking sentimentally about being part of the *werin*.

Other research also points to the significance of institutional religion, respectability and class. Skeggs (1997) argues that 'respectability is one of the most ubiquitous signifiers of class' (68) and is 'central' to the development of English identity (124), and I would also argue that it is central to Welsh identity. In Chapter 4 I explored how the church, historically, has played a significant role in creating a repressed and respectable identity for women; however, the church still plays a part in conferring respectability, particularly within its rituals. Fenton (2014) for example, argues that engagement with the church and its ceremonies, especially baptism, is a way of gaining respectability (as a form of accruing symbolic capital) for those living in working-class communities in the northeast of England.

An important finding from this research is that there are new constructed Welsh identities emerging, and as religion diminishes as an influence, there is a danger that in its place Welsh identity could be controlled and constructed by a minority within the Welsh middle class to the exclusion of most of the people of Wales. A worrying feature of this identity construction is the appropriation of working-class symbols and stories and the rejection of groups of people who are not 'Welsh enough'. It is, essentially, an identity based on exclusion and utilising a newer form of shaming.

Another key issue raised by this research is that there are significant differences in how the different generations engage with religion and identity, and in fact any form of authority and community activity. One way of understanding the findings from this project is the concept of the 'subjective turn'.

The subjective turn

This study shows that middle-aged and younger women are increasingly rejecting an institutional Christianity which fails to acknowledge or represent their values or to encourage their empowerment and agency.

The women represented in my study were mainly middle-aged and demonstrated a decisive shift in religious observance and influence between the generations. They reported that for their own mothers, institutional religion had formed a crucial part of their figured worlds, but that they themselves were now rejecting this, particularly as an influence on morality. In fact, the churches were severely criticised for hypocrisy and even the women who were committed churchgoers revealed that institutional religion was almost irrelevant to their faith lives and especially to their decisions about behaviour or doctrine. This indicates that it would be productive to investigate further the experiences of younger women and girls and the role of religion within their identity.

Arnett (2014) argues that the features of the figured worlds of those he calls 'emerging adults' are radically different from previous generations and that their focus is on identity exploration and self-fulfilment (Arnett, 2014: 563). Although Arnett's work is based on research in the US, it does have some relevance to Wales given the Western context. He found that young people's attitudes to religion was highly diverse, from those who are hostile to religion to those who are conservative believers (Arnett, 2014: 4574); however, traditional religion and institutions are unattractive to emerging adults, particularly in their focus on social events and regular gatherings, which was a significant part of the lives of those who are in the older generations today. Arnett writes:

> Even if the format changed, participating in religious services would have limited appeal to most emerging adults, precisely because it is, by definition, a collective rather than an individual expression of faith. Participation in a religious institution, even a liberal one, requires them to abide by a certain set of beliefs and rules and therefore constitutes an intolerable compromise of their individuality. (Arnett, 2014: 4663–77)

The different generations have distinctive values, practices and cultural norms and assumptions. The women in my sample exemplified the 'subjective turn' in their relationship with faith and institutional religion (Heelas and Woodhead, 2005: 2–5). Although some form of spirituality and a moral framework were important to every participant, whether or not they were a believer in God or part of a religious institution,[31] even the women who were fully committed to their denominations made their own decisions about matters of faith and morality. There was no sense that any woman whose work I read or who spoke to me accepted uncritically the teachings of their churches, or, for that matter, the cultural Nonconformist Christianity that they had been socialised into or they regarded as an integral aspect of Welsh female identity. It was salient only in that they described their own identity in opposition to it.

When women had faith it was a faith of their own (Beck, 2010) unregulated by church or spiritual leaders. Marged and Sera, for example, would ascribe their empowerment to their personal relationship with God; yet this experience was unrelated to their experience of church or institutional life. I found in some of the women a longing for a real and transformative faith sustained and nourished by church life. Yet their experience of institutionalised pastoral care and leadership was inconsistent – there were some significant examples of supportive localised pastoral care alongside poor experiences of misogyny and disempowerment. One important finding arising from this project is that it seems that churches have had little impact on the spiritual lives of the women and are irrelevant to them.

Heelas and Woodhead describe what the subjective turn might mean for those living in the West in the modern (or the postmodern) era in that we regard ourselves as being our own authority, rather than having any sense that we have to 'defer' to a 'higher authority' (Heelas and Woodhead, 2005: 4). They describe a shift towards subjectivity and the centrality of the individual, their choices and their development within society whether it is within education, consumerism or work culture:

> Each of these shifts involves a turn away from a more hierarchical, deferential, life-as [living according to external expectations] order of things in which the teacher, the shop-keeper, the doctor, the manager was 'god'. (Heelas and Woodhead, 2005: 5)

Ominously, they describe how organisations which have not caught up with this change in society will increasingly find themselves 'out of step with the times' (Heelas and Woodhead, 2005: 5). This was the lifeworld of the women I interviewed and this was also their approach to religion. They skilfully held a variety of practices, values and influences in tension and were confident in being able to appropriate what they found helpful within the tradition and reject what was unhelpful.

Although religion was seen as a carrier of national identity, with 'chapel' being seen as more Welsh than 'church', women's relationships with religious institutions were tangential. When women had individual faith, this had been a factor in their self-confidence though those who were not Christians were also similarly agentic. In some cases however, experience of church life had been oppressive, damaging and misogynistic.

In terms of individualised faith, the God encountered in their own spiritual experiences was different from the God of the institutions. For example, the women reported that they had had strength to divorce their husbands, or accept their lesbianism as coming from God, whereas the church's teaching (although admittedly in a state of flux)[32] was that both divorce and homosexuality were wrong. There is a dissonance between official church teaching and the individual beliefs of women in Wales, particularly in terms of sexuality and relationships.

Middle-aged and younger women in Wales are looking for a new understanding of sex and gender, more in tune with their experience and values. Given that theologies of gender are changing, is it possible to enrich our understanding of what it means to be human with a theology which is more affirming and empowering for women?

A new theology of sex and gender

In fact, it is disingenuous to suggest that a theology of the human person has remained constant, particularly with reference to sex and sexuality (see Jones and Yarhouse, 2006: 135), given that Christian teaching has varied considerably across the past two millennia and has been informed by the different and developing ideas of the cultures in which these discussions have been situated (World Council of Churches, 2005: 11).

The binary male–female distinction within gender and sex is a modern invention and until the eighteenth century in Western thought it was assumed there was only one real sex: male (Thatcher, 2016: 1). To read into the scriptures and early Christian writings an idea of two and opposite sexes is anachronistic. The Early Church Fathers regarded the *imago dei* as found not in the embodied person but rather in the reason or the soul, and in women only imperfectly in as much as they too have a soul (Gonzalez, 2007: 707–15). Because women were seen as closer to the body, this somehow led to them being an inferior version of the image of God and to be viewed as flawed men (Gonzales, 2007: 84).

Furthermore, according to Augustine, women could not fully reflect God's image in themselves alone, but only in relationship to a man (Gonzalez, 2007: 889). Women were created inferior and their role was to complement men in enabling sexual relationships and procreation (Ruether, 1999: 101). He also argued that this difference in how men and women were perceived was always part of God's plan in creation and that the Fall had resulted in the further subordination of women as a 'special punishment for sin' (Ruether, 1999: 101).

However, this would not last for eternity: the future heavenly world would mean that this subordination would finally be overcome, for women as well as men (Ruether, 1999: 101). Similarly, for Thomas Aquinas, Aristotelian biology pointed to women as inferior and inadequate versions of men (Gonzalez, 2007: 999). Because of women's roles as subordinate helpmeets, women and men did not reflect God's image equally (Gonzalez, 2007: 997).

Thatcher argues that to read binary sex into scripture is a form of 'presentism', that is a 'tendency to introduce present-day assumptions and ideas into analyses and interpretations of the past' (Thatcher, 2016: 84). He elaborates that debates against the ordination of women are based on both a one-sex model (women as inferior males) in parallel with a complementarian two-sex model where male and female roles are essentially and qualitatively different (Thatcher, 2016: 87–95). However, there are other ways of understanding sex and gender theologically.

The Trinity and personal identity

Volf, whom we have already discussed in terms of theological approaches to identity, argues for a theology of the human person which is based on a Trinitarian understanding of being made in God's image. He regards biblical descriptions of maleness and femaleness as so culturally conditioned that they are of limited value for other contexts because they contain particular cultural values about gender and sexuality as identity and roles (Volf, 1996: 182). In fact, any essentialist proposals about masculinity and femininity would, he maintains be 'harmful' and 'inadmissibly freeze a particular cultural understanding of gender identity and seek to impose it inappropriately in changing situations' (182).

Looking through the lens of Galatians 3: 28, where the apostle Paul proclaims that there is no Jew, Gentile, male, female, slave or free because all are one in Christ, Volf sees the sexes as not oppositional, nor rendered sexless or spiritualised out of sexed bodies, but as indwelling, interrelated and dynamic. As the Trinity is persons indwelling, self-giving, open to the other, so is the potential for human relations (189). In other words because God is Trinity, human beings are not a duality of male and female, but have a non-essential particularised identity which is fluid, relational and open to the other, not in opposition to it.

The Pauline epistles speak of a new understanding of difference within social identities, in the Spirit, in the body of Christ and in Christ. In the Spirit, identity becomes destabilised and freed from social expectations and roles:

> The Spirit does not erase bodily inscribed differences, but allows access into the one body of Christ to the people with such differences on the same terms. What the Spirit does erase (or at least loosen) is a stable and socially constructed correlation between social differences and social roles. The gifts of the Spirit are given irrespective of such differences. Against the cultural expectation that women be silent and submit to men, in Pauline communities they speak and lead because the Spirit gives them gifts to speak and lead. (Volf, 1996: 48)

He is critical of the desire for a bounded identity as exclusionary, and although 'the tension between the self and the other is built into the very desire for identity' (91) this is challenged by the Christian faith. For example, inclusion is at the heart of the Eucharist where there is communion between God and his people and people with each other, where the body and blood of Christ is literally taken in by the believers to become a part of themselves and members of the church become members of one body and made into a new creation (129, 130).

Volf's work shows that a credible (and for me persuasive) case can be made for a theology of the human person which is non-essentialist, affirms the full role and humanity of women and allows for homosexual as well as heterosexual committed relationships within its sexual ethics, and this is rooted in a contextual and contemporary understanding of God as Trinity. This opens the way to a more inclusive understanding of sexuality and gender which could be utilised by the churches in Wales today. Therefore, if Christian teaching can develop in order to be more empowering for Welsh women, similarly is there a challenge to the churches in their practice?

The end of care and control

It is not only in Wales that the churches have exercised considerable influence. British culture has largely been shaped by Christianity (Davie, 2015: 3) and its influence can still be seen in art, literature and music, disciplines which cannot be fully understood apart from this Christian historical context (72). Davie speaks of perceptions of the Church as a 'public utility' (82) which was also my experience as a vicar, where parishioners would often express surprise that their taxes did not contribute to the running of the church and graveyard in their village. Despite growing unbelief and secularism, people in Britain as well as Wales still turn to the Church for various rituals at the time of birth, marriage and death (82).

This study points to a declining influence of religion on women in Wales, however, given that there remains a residual influence for the moment, what role should the churches exercise within the lives of women and men today in Wales? What does the Strong Woman have to say to the religious institutions which attempted and failed to control her? The answer, I believe, lies in a new identity for the churches and the end of what I would term 'care and control'.

When I was first ordained, in 1994, ministry was predominantly about pastoral care and particularly pastoral visiting. My training had included listening skills and one of the reasons why I was attracted to the ministry was because I wanted to 'help people'. As a curate, I would be given weekly lists of names of people to visit. The previous rector had had a strict regime of visiting where he called in on every single household in the parish for ten minutes each every six months and made notes about them in small black notebooks. He was known as a driven, prickly but charismatic man – it is difficult to imagine that his visits were universally welcomed.

Our own visiting schedule was less punishing: lists of housebound people and care homes which three clergy would take in turns to visit each month with communion, those who were ill or bereaved and, if we had the time, members who were on the electoral roll. Some of the names given to me were clearly generous benefactors who had donated money in the past because of the persistence of the previous rector. However many of these rich elderly women did not want to have to make small talk with a young female deacon: one woman would not allow me in through her garden gate because she did not agree with female clergy, and another let me into her house, sat me down but then went off to the kitchen for an hour and, when a cup of tea was slow to materialise, I let myself out quietly through the front door.

However most of the people on the list, if they were well, always had a cake in the tin in case anyone called, and the best china was even brought out for the curate. The front room was always tidy for visitors. I learnt that parish visiting meant listening to stories about grandchildren and gossip about the clergy and parishioners. Many of the people I visited were lonely and were grateful of an hour or so to talk about their own lives.

This parish visiting was the bedrock of ministry in the last century, supported by the apocryphal saying 'a home-going parson makes a churchgoing people'. However it was based on a condescending model, not only the priest or pastor as father-knows-best, but also the pattern set by middle-class ladies in the nineteenth century calling on the 'deserving poor' in order to provide encouragement and to 'do good' (Burgess, 2000: 38).

If the role of the church was to put love of neighbour into action, this was a highly systematised approach. In this model, love is not a mutual exercise, but one person is the provider, the professional expert Christian, and others are the consumers of this ministry. This model, I would argue, has led to the passivity I mentioned in Chapter 7 that is endemic in the Church in Wales.

As we have seen, the subjective turn as well as the practices and discourses of shaming mean that church as care and control will be unattractive to middle-aged and younger generations. Is it inevitable that the institutional church is hierarchical, ordered and infantilising or is it possible for mutuality and empowerment to be at the heart of church governance and practice?

Mitchell (2011) argues that the Christendom model which has been so influential within Western Christianity is deeply flawed. With the conversion of Constantine, the Roman emperor, to Christianity and the spread of Christianity within the Western world, Church and empire became synonymous with hierarchy, power and control by the few for the benefit of the few. Church organisation, practice and teaching became subsumed by a political exercise of sovereign power, at first through monarchy and then the nation-state.

Ironically, a religion of self-giving love as seen in the life of Christ, who himself critiqued the use and abuse of religious power, becomes a religion which promotes imperialism. This leads Mitchell to question whether the Church can address its own marginalisation within society in the UK unless it disentangles itself from the establishment, and critiques its prior involvement with imperial power (Mitchell, 2011).

Hull further argues that the Church has wrongly focussed its energies on worship and shaming rather than having a positive role within society:

> Because of the Church's concentration upon its own life and its isolation from the mission of God that called it into being, the Church itself becomes a fetish. The theology of justice and peace is replaced by an orifice theology concerned with what comes in or out of the bodily orifices: sex, speech and sacraments. (Hull, 2014: 4754)

There is a task ahead of 'disentangling' Christian teaching from the imperialist overlayers of the past in order to get to Jesus' message of love (Hull, 2014: 4623).

It could also be argued in our era that some of the renewed emphasis on evangelism and mission is not so much a concern for the flourishing of individuals and communities and for their spiritual growth and relationship with the divine but an anxiety about wanting to return the church to a 'Christendom' model in order to reclaim its former authority and power (Hull, 2006: 20; see also Pattison, 2008: 7–10). However, strategies and modern practices or worship fail to address the deeper issue of the rejection of many people of the institutional Church precisely because of the controlling and dominating nature of churches on a local and national level. If churches want to play a part in the lives of men and women, they need to develop an altogether humbler identity.

As Heelas and Woodhead (2005) maintain, the individualistic (post)modern Western world is not simply anarchic. People's working lives are tightly controlled and managed (Heelas and Woodhead, 2005: 128). If church life continues to be hierarchical and controlled (albeit in a different way) this will not be attractive to those who are seeking to escape from the bureaucracy and regimentation of professions such as education, social work and medicine (Heelas and Woodhead, 2005: 128). It is not simply that church buildings and artefacts are alien to middle-aged and younger generations; church discourses, practices and expectations are similarly confusing and strange. Heelas and Woodhead state:

> In a nutshell, our argument is that churches and chapels have suffered because many people are simply no longer willing to submit to the roles, duties, rituals, traditions, offices and expectations which these institutions impose ... the congregational domain continues to be populated by those who favour life-as [living according to external expectations] and has failed to widen its appeal to those more influenced by the subjective turn. (Heelas and Woodhead, 2005: 112)

Unless churches can find new ways of addressing the spiritual and other needs of individuals and their communities, they will find that they are increasingly ignored.

The different denominations face different but connected challenges in twenty-first-century Wales. All the churches face an image problem; however the Free Churches, more than other churches, still suffer from the repressive and repressed stereotypes of the past. Social media and other forms of communication offer an opportunity for churches to promote positive stories about engagement with communities and more imaginative and creative worship. Challenging perceptions of chapels as dreary places, isolated from their communities, is an urgent task.

Likewise, for Anglican and Catholic churches which have a more hierarchical image, having a more inclusive and egalitarian approach will be important in order to be able to communicate with middle-aged and younger people who have a much less deferential and a far more participatory style of engaging with organisations and institutions. The way in which the churches will make an impact is through a myriad of daily encounters in ordinary communities across Wales. If faith and love is seen to be put into practice by churches across the land they may even earn a place again in the hearts of the Welsh people.

Conclusion: emerging Welsh identities

In this book I have explored the nature and extent of the impact of the dominant religious traditions of Wales on the identity of Welsh women through engaging with different conversation partners. I have found identity to be a useful term with which to explore how we feel about ourselves and the social groupings to which we belong. I have used several theoretical lenses through which to understand identity and have located the discussion within a postmodern understanding of identity as performed and constructed in discourse, often for political reasons. The work of Castells (2010), who argues that it is possible for identities to be constructed to resist the dominant identities, is particularly helpful in understanding the Welsh context.

Another conversation partner has been the theologian Miroslav Volf who also utilises a postmodern view of identity in order to inform his theology of the human person. He admits that the church has 'malfunctioned' in its teaching and living out of the gospel, leading to oppression rather than the flourishing of human beings, particularly with regard to gender and sex. His Trinitarian theology of embrace rather than exclusion and critique of 'othering' within identity is a challenge for the churches to encourage men and women to fulfil their potential rather than be restricted by gender norms or other forms of essentialising.

A brief historical survey of the relationship between religion and Welsh identity since the seventeenth century shows that the relationship between Welsh identity and religion has been controversial and contested and that certain denominations at different times have claimed to be more supportive of Welsh traditions and more Welsh than the others. Female Welsh identity has been particularly susceptible to political construction. The churches, their leaders and politicians have utilised religious practices and values in order to construct an oppressive resistance identity for women in particular to withstand the dominance of a genteel Englishness and its critique of the uncivilised nature of the people of Wales.

This identity found expression in a chapel-going, God-fearing stereotype, with an accompanying pressure to be respectable, as a form of stratification and inclusion in society. This is a familiar discourse for middle-aged and older people living in Wales as they reflect on their upbringing. However, the different generations exhibit a distinctive response: this is the figured world of older people, whereas middle-aged and younger people have constructed their identities in opposition to this or reject it altogether. It would be interesting to explore further what Welsh people now use to construct their identities – and, in particular, the role of the Welsh language. One worrying aspect was identified by my research participants however, a middle-class exclusive approach to Welsh identity which appropriated Welsh working-class symbols and stories whilst alienating those they did not consider to be 'Welsh' enough.

My empirical study, comprising of an examination of Welsh women's writing along with thirteen research conversations, portrays a new and emerging Wales. Faith and religion are in the process of becoming separated from social identity and a new Welsh identity, disconnected from religion, and particular cultural expressions is developing within the context of the Western subjective turn. The resistance identities constructed for women, of which religion was a major part, are now being deconstructed by Welsh women themselves. The effect of religion on identity in Welsh women is therefore in transition and is generation-specific.

The writings, life stories and interviews revealed that many of the women have been influenced by religion, especially during their childhood, and that they saw Christianity, predominantly in its Free Church form, as an important part of Welsh identity. However personal faith (if they had a faith) was significantly more important to them than institutional religion and some women had experienced misogyny and oppression by the Church and Christian organisations.

Despite my initial assumption that Welsh women have negative self-perceptions, the findings of the study are that there is a salient and potent archetype for Welsh women of the Strong Woman, as well as a long history of Welsh women's writing which has articulated a passionate and embodied faith and relationship with the divine. Laughter and humour have also been shown to be an important dissenting discourse. These aspects of Welsh female social identity could form the basis of a new and empowered identity.

The influence of religion on the identity of Welsh women, though historically strong, is now diminishing at a significant rate with each generation. Different age groups are living in different figured worlds with distinctive practices, discourses and assumptions. I end with a call for the churches in Wales to be more concerned for the flourishing of individuals and communities, and to put faith into practice in concrete ways rather than wanting to return the church to its former powerful position in society. The damaging effect of religious power within a culture can be seen in the recent socio-religious history of Wales, in particular, the oppressive practices developed by the churches in response to the Blue Books' report in the mid-nineteenth century.

In conclusion, the churches in Wales need to engage with the reality of women's and men's lives if they are to be spaces for women and men, of all generations, to encounter the divine and each other. Not only does this mean attending to the subtle forms of stratification and practices which continue to shame and stigmatise, but also laying aside theologies of identity which seek to control, and, instead, embracing theologies and practices which empower and encourage people to find God for themselves and to live out a meaningful and active faith in the world. In any case, the women in this study have shown that they are well able to find spiritual meaning within or without institutional forms of Christianity. If churches want to engage with middle-aged and younger women they will need to do so on their terms and be willing to allow church culture to be transformed by them. It is a call to humility and courage, to the discernment of a new vocation. Can the churches bear to lose their former influential role in order to find a new role once again? This is the challenge of the Strong Woman.

Appendix: Research Methods

Introduction

I have already mentioned in the introduction that my methodology utilises a practical theology 'critical conversation' approach. Unlike traditional qualitative research, where the literary review is seen as providing a background for empirical work, a critical conversation regards all information-gathering as part of the research method, part of the 'conversation'. However, it was important to listen to the distinctive voices of Welsh women; therefore conducting my own original research was an important part of this exploration. I now explain in more detail my methods.

A qualitative framework

Qualitative research is now established as an appropriate methodology for empirical investigation.[33] This approach could be said to be more consonant with the turn to language, the particular and the local, found in science at the beginning of the postmodern period (Flick, 2014: 960) and an acceptance that knowledge can be gained from both particular cases (ideographic)[34] and approaches which look at general laws (nomothetic) (Swinton and Mowat, 2006: 44).

The difference between qualitative and quantitative research is more usually described as a distinction between 'approaches which are concerned with number, measurement and quantification, on the one hand and those which are concerned with meanings and the relationships between meanings on the other' (Slee, 2004: 9–10). However Creswell (2009: 3) maintains that the difference between the approaches is not simply between forms of data collection and analysis, but also the philosophical assumptions that researchers bring to their project.

Questions of identity, belonging and the impact of religious teaching and institutions on culture fit naturally into a qualitative research framework. This approach does not see the world as 'out there' but as experienced and interpreted by social actors, including myself as researcher. Its home is within a constructivist paradigm, where 'truth' is not external and waiting to be identified, but is constructed between participants within the social world (Swinton and Mowat, 2006: 33) and can be discovered in unique experiences (Swinton and Mowat, 2006: 43). The validity of the fieldwork is not gained from the possibility of replicating the data elsewhere or drawing generalisations from it, although find-ings that can be applied more widely ('resonance') strengthen the validity (Swin-ton and Mowat, 2006: 47).

Although the nature of qualitative research is not easy to define given its constantly evolving and complex nature (Denzin and Lincoln, 2011: xiii; Creswell, 2013: 42), many scholars agree that there are certain features held in common:

- the centrality of the perspectives, interpretation and meaning of the research participants themselves, studied in their natural setting (Creswell, 2013: 45, 47)
- that research is about gaining knowledge which can be used to 'empower' participants or members of a social group and learn from their stories (Creswell, 2013: 48)
- the importance of the reflexivity of the researcher (Flick, 2014: 857; Creswell, 2013: 47): the researcher is a key 'instrument' within the research (Creswell, 2013: 45)
- the value of interdisciplinary work and the utilisation of a variety of meth-ods and data in order to gain a rich, in-depth understanding (Denzin and Lincoln, 2011: 6, Creswell, 2013: 45)
- that the analysis as well as the practice of research can be messy and complex with a dynamic moving in between 'inductive and deductive' logic and between themes and the data (Creswell, 2013: 47)
- finally, there is a close link between the methods, the theories that lie behind them and their relevance to the particular subject being studied (Flick, 2014: 805)

The emphasis of my own project on reflexivity, utilising different and interdisci-plinary methods, studying the meaning and interpretation of the research partici-pant herself in a 'natural' setting and a desire to allow Welsh women's voices and stories to be heard means that this project is ideally located within a qualitative approach which regards researcher reflexivity[35] and a variety of approaches as strengths. An aspect of this reflexivity is to clarify the social and epistemological position of the researcher.

Reflexivity and research

The role of the researcher

Both Practical Theology and feminist methodologies acknowledge the impor-tance of the researcher and their own story, standpoint and commitments. Reflex-ivity is a 'primary tool' with which to access and understand the meaning garnered from empirical research (Swinton and Mowat, 2006: 59). However, does this mean that the researcher is 'biased' and raises the question of whether this affects the findings? Feminist approaches have challenged the idea that there is such a thing as an 'impartial' methodology, one that prevents the researcher 'from contaminating the data' (England, 1994: 81; Davies, 1999: 3), and contested the ethics of the belief that it is possible to look at other human beings with a neutral objective gaze (England, 1994: 82). Furthermore researcher involvement is seen positively by qualitative researchers. Oakley, quoted by Shooter states:

> … personal involvement is more than dangerous bias – it is the condition under which people come to know each other and to admit others into their lives. (Oakley in Shooter, 2012: 38)

In order to preserve the integrity of the research it was important to have high standards of reflexivity in order to guard against influencing the data unduly (Ribbens and Edwards, 1998: 4). This included making explicit my own position, being intentional about reflecting on the power dynamic inherent in my own social identities and roles (Swinton and Mowat, 2006: 64, 65), and reflecting throughout the research and critiquing my practice (Swinton and Mowat, 2006: 66).

The characteristics of reflective research

A constant deliberation on the experience of research and the interpretation of it is a key feature of reflective research (Alvesson and Skoldberg 2009: 9). Within this methodology, data is problematised, placed in context and explored from different perspectives of experience, theory, language and culture (Alvesson and Skoldberg, 2009: 9).

Slee (2004) elaborates on what she considers to be elements in reflective research as well as characteristic aspects of feminist research:

- the research process is conducted and written about in a transparent way
- the researcher writes in the first person
- is clear about her own commitments
- is honest about the 'messiness' of the process for example in allowing mistakes and dead ends to be written about in the text
- reflects how her position throughout the research has changed
- is aware of and writes about her own feelings as well as thought and acknowledges 'affectivity as a major resource in knowing'. (Slee, 2004: 52)

Slee argues that this brings integrity to the research process and is about creating a new set of conventions as to how to conduct and write about empirical work (Slee, 2004: 52). These have also influenced my own research design and practice.

However, in reflective research, it is not only the data and its interpretation of it that is explored in depth: the role of the researcher herself is also a site for study. Part of the honesty and transparency of my reflexive approach is to clarify my own commitments.

The researcher as reflective writer and poet

A 'reflection in action' approach is considered an aspect of good empirical research practice (Bold, 2012: 3). I have used writing as a form of capturing and stimulating reflection during different parts of the research, as appropriate; I have kept a research journal and a blog[36] and have also written separate reflections on the process of interviewing each participant. In reality I found it difficult to commit to writing the journal regularly and therefore the blog and other forms of writing have been important aspects of my reflective writing.

Another way in which I have developed my reflexive skills is through poetry, and I decided that I could utilise this both in reflecting on the research process and investigating my own experience and the experiences of others. Poetry can access untapped reflections on situations, for example, in noticing concrete particularity, or relevant metaphors or imaginative connections. My poems reflect my particular point of view, emotions and thoughts at any particular time during the research and I have used my poetry throughout the book in order to make my assumptions and thoughts as transparent as possible, as well as to provide a depth to my reflection.

I started the research with the view that women in Wales found religion to be ambivalent, if not negative, to their sense of well-being and self-esteem, and was influenced by the mythology of Welsh Nonconformist culture as 'oppressive'. In the early part of the research I wrote a poem (which is rather polemical), exploring my own feelings about the histories of Ann Griffiths the hymn-writer and Gwerful Mechain, the poet whose work I mentioned in Chapter 4. Both women known for their passionate, even sexual writing about the Godhead, and I contrasted this with the current state of religion in Wales, with the resonant symbols of mantelpieces with ornaments and chapel furniture. As a result of this I wrote the poem *Daughters of Gwerful Mechain* which is at the end of Chapter 7.

This poem reflects the sense of anger and frustration I felt with institutional religion at the time and an attempt to think through ideas of faith and embodiment from a Welsh perspective. There is attention here to the resonant objects and buildings of Wales – chapels, brasses, ornaments, front parlours; all still prevalent features of present-day chapel buildings and the homes of older people living in more traditional communities.

My later reading involved looking at the theology and sociology of objects and what they tell us about our society (Hurdley, 2013). Therefore, this poem enabled me to reflect not just on my learning but also to notice the concrete elements of identity in a way I would not have been able to access otherwise. However, the interest for me now, having written up my research, is to notice how my position has changed. I use the poem in Chapter 7 not as a call to empowerment, which was my original intention in the poem, but as a celebration of the agency and confidence that I found amongst the women I interviewed or read.

Similarly, at the beginning of the research process I felt unsure and inadequate (the 'impostorship' I mentioned in the introduction). I wrote 'Theology Seminar' (see Chapter 2) after attending one of my first seminars, articulating my hesitancy and beginning to find a voice and a new vocabulary, and noticing this in another student.

The poem articulates the ambivalence for female researchers, again a sense of alienation and a self-perception of not 'belonging' within academic circles. Since writing this poem and attending my first seminars I have had to learn a new vocabulary and I have now begun to use some of these unfamiliar words. Although the poem does not state this explicitly, it looks towards a new stage in the researcher's academic journey, when she feels comfortable in this new discourse and will not need validation from the confident male academic with the signifiers of male power and formality – the tie and beard.

I suggest that the validity of this project can be derived from the fact that my own perspective changed during the research process. In order to underline my commitment to be transparent I now outline my location as a researcher.

My commitments as a researcher

A feminist commitment

A feminist perspective shares the concerns and issues of Practical Theology in that it is also transdisciplinary, transformative and participatory and has a special concern with the researcher playing a key part in the process (Reinharz, 1992: 240). It uses a variety of methods (Reinharz, 1992: 243) and seeks both to identify and ameliorate the power dynamic between researcher and researched through both personal involvement and the creation of rapport, even friendship (Reinharz, 1992: 263). Feminist research has a special concern for the marginalised, and for giving them and also the researcher herself 'a voice' (Reinharz 1992:16). Research is not necessarily feminist because it is interested in issues of gender, however, feminist research can be defined as such if it is informed by feminist theory and has as an aim the transformation of the lives of women, for justice and empowerment (Ramazonoglu, 2002: 147).

Given that feminist research is defined in different ways by different feminists (Reinharz, 192: 6), it is important for me to clarify what I mean by this stance. For me, the specific characteristics of feminist research are that there is:

- a foregrounding of female experience as a corrective to the emphasis on traditional research on the male as 'norm' (Slee, 2004: 46)
- an attendance to the power dynamic inherent in any form of human interaction and an acceptance that this will also be true of the research process (Slee, 2004: 43)
- a commitment to make space for women's voices to be heard directly (Slee, 2004: 43)
- an attempt to make research practices as non-oppressive as possible (Slee, 2004: 50)

- a commitment to transparency and reflexivity as key characteristics of the process (Slee, 2004: 5; Reinharz, 1992: 258)
- an acknowledegment of the importance of empathy and complete attentiveness to the perspective of the research participant (Slee, 2004: 44; Phillips, 2011: 60)
- a refusal to accept the traditional dichotomies between lay and expert, professional and client and to see those who are being researched as participants in the process[37] (Slee, 2004: 44; Reinharz, 1992: 263)
- an acceptance of my own involvement in the research process,[38] that I also have a contribution to make (it would be patronising as well as inaccurate to suggest that my interviewees are the 'real experts' when I also am a member of the group of people I am studying) (Reinharz, 1992: 16, 258)
- a desire for research to play a part in empowering women and transform communities and societies (Reinharz, 1992: 251)

These, along with the characteristics of reflective research identified by Slee (2004), have been the principles that have guided the design and practice of the empirical aspect of my investigation.

Research design

Choosing the right method

Practitioners maintain that the use of a narrative methodology is particularly appropriate for research on individual and social identity (Riessman, 1993: 5). Biography forms a very important part of identity (Giddens, 1991: 55) and even if we question the idea of an essentialised unchanging self, it is still possible and productive to speak of a 'narrative identity' as something that is relatively stable and coherent (Elliott, 2005: 1) or even creates this sense of coherence (Linde, 1999: 1; Loseke, 2007: 672). The recounting of a life story, however, involves not only a person listing events, but is also an interpretation of those events. Narratives are not just individualistic and personal – stories can also help construct 'cultural identities' in terms of producing stereotypes and common discourses (Loseke, 2007: 661; Riessman, 1993: 5).

Wodak, de Cillia, Reisigl and Liebhart (2009), following Ricoeur, see narrative identity as a helpful concept, reflecting both the shifting nature of identity and the significance of a life story in holding an individual's identity together (2009: 15). This can also be enlarged to include an examination of national identity: Uri Ram, with reference to Geertz, agrees in commenting that 'Nationality is a narration, a story which people tell about themselves in order to lend meaning to their social world' (Wodak, de Cillia, Reisigl and Liebhart, 2009: 23). Both narrative and discourse (and their relationship) are therefore highly significant in the construction of a national identity.

The strong relationship between story, Wales and theology were persuasive arguments for me as to why a narrative approach could be useful in looking at the identity of women in Wales within the discipline of Practical Theology and I decided to interview a small sample of women about their life stories using this methodology, as well as examine a sample of memoirs.

Narrative research

Introduction

> Telling a life story is like telling a sacred story. (Atkinson, 1998: 14)

Narrative methodology is a vast subject, incorporating the analysis of images and objects as well as texts and spoken words. It would be more accurate to characterise my research as a narrative approach rather than narrative analysis given that I decided not to study texts in linguistic detail (for example as in Labovian analysis), but rather concentrate on the 'told' rather than the 'telling' (Riessman, 2008: 54) for data collection.

Narrative research, it is argued, is both useful for studies on individuals[39] and on groups (Riessman, 1993: 5). If narratives construct personal identity in a postmodern world, they can also help construct group, cultural and national identity (Riessman, 2008: 7). This approach is therefore ideal for a project that studies identity from a personal and social perspective (Linde, 1993: 3).

Stories can be important in constructing group identities and are particularly effective in highlighting political issues, as certain stories can represent the stories of others who share that identity (Plummer, 2001). There are political implications as to how and whose story is utilised – for example, the discussion of why the respectably married Rosa Parks's refusal to give away her bus seat to a white person was chosen over the story of the unmarried pregnant teenager Claudette Colvin's identical action within the civil rights movement in America (Lovell, 2003).

As I have explained in the introduction, significance is given to stories within the research encounter (Mishler, 1986: 5, 69). Although storytelling is an interpretive act for the storyteller, meaning is also constructed between interviewer and interviewee (Mishler, 1986: 52; Squire, 2008: 44).[40] In each retelling the circumstances and experience of the story are different (Squire, 2008: 44). In other words, narratives are both reconstructed and co-constructed (Squire, 2008: 45; Salmon and Riessman, 2008: 80). As an 'ordinary' human activity, reflecting on narratives within research is a 'human process', albeit using some specialist tools, but it is nevertheless an 'encounter' (Elliott, 2005: 36). Furthermore Mishler argues for a more explicit acknowledgement of how the analysis is based on 'everyday contextual understandings' (Mishler, 1986: 5).

Telling a story is an interpretation of the past and, unlike historical research, in narrative research there is no 'canonical' interpretation or validation of this method. The storyteller is her own interpreter and validator (Riessman, 2002: 706). Although 'coherence' (Linde, 1993) can be a key interpretive feature of narratives, for the narrator it is also true that the identities re-presented in story form, as well as the narratives themselves can be fragmentary and incoherent due to the nature of the suffering and pain that is involved in some stories (Salmon and Riessman, 2008: 84). As a form of interviewing it is entirely consonant with the feminist standpoint I have already outlined.

Narrative strategies

In order to explore this methodology I conducted a number of pilot interviews. I asked several women who were attending a spirituality day to fill in question-naires on their own histories and the effect of religion on their biographies. I found that asking such personal questions in an impersonal way did not yield much data and I was unable to follow up on questions with them as we were following a rigid schedule of questions.

I then followed a semi-structured approach and interviewed three women, one alone and two together, about their lives and how religion had affected it. This helped me to formulate three questions which I then used to interview another woman, and with her attempted to write a story of her life. The narrative was fascinating; however I wrote it up in the third person and gained her permission and her approval for every part of the subsequent story. This empowered her and she found the experience moving, as I did. However, the resulting 'story', written in the third person, seemed impersonal and did not reflect the energy and sponta-neity of the encounter.

To test whether the story was more effective written completely by the partici-pant I asked an acquaintance to write her own story in a few thousand words. Again, this yielded interesting information but because I was totally uninvolved with the production of this story, I was unable to follow up with questions which would have yielded further valuable data.

This led me to decide that I would conduct interviews in a semi-structured way, with a few common questions, but with considerable freedom to ask follow up questions as well as seek clarifications. Following Mishler (1986) and Slee (2004) my approach was to try and ameliorate the power dynamic between researcher and researched and to attempt to put equality as well as empathy and friendship at the heart of each encounter.

Sampling

Choosing research participants for this project was problematic, as the project could be critiqued for not having a broad enough range, or for not being purpose-ful enough in choosing people with various social identities in order to generalise from my findings. I would argue that within a qualitative and a feminist frame-work (for example, see Plaskow and Christ, 1989, there is value in exploring women's individual stories),[41] and narrative researchers also, similarly, maintain that deep reflection on individual stories help us understand general human expe-riences better (Wengraf, 2000: 161).

I have explained some of my decisions regarding sampling in the introduction. I would want to elaborate on this by saying that I also made initial enquiries through a Muslim contact in order to explore the possibility of interviewing Muslim women; however, this proved difficult to set up, especially as I was based in north Wales. My contact was not confident that he would be able to find anyone in this age group based in north Wales who had been born and brought up in Wales (though he was aware of several Muslim women who had moved into the area relatively recently), and, in the end, we failed to set up a meeting, although it would have been possible for me to interview someone in south Wales.

The interviews took place in a variety of locations – neutral premises, my home or the home or workplace of the participant. All the participants were given a pseudonym or chose one for themselves. They were sent a letter or email outlining the project and before each interview I read out the letter and gained their consent. For example, the letter and consent form stated that the interview would be recorded and transcribed, that they were welcome to make changes to the transcript and that details would be anonymised and the conversations kept confidential. I explained the procedure of analysis and that the data could potentially be published in various forms. I also explained that they had the right to speak for as long as they wanted, about what they wanted as well as to refuse to answer questions and withdraw at any time. I also explained that I would keep a separate form with their pseudonym as well as noting where they had lived and which denominations they had been members of at different stages in their lives.

After the interview I wrote up reflections (which I did not share with the participant), however, I sent them a draft transcript and invited them to make any changes they wished. Some participants did not want to change their transcript or even be given the opportunity to read it. One participant asked for some changes in order that she would not be identified. I also took great care over anonymising the interviews and I gained permission from one participant for her transcript to be used in full in the appendix to my original thesis. I was aware that in handling the interview transcripts my commitment both to transparency and to non-oppressive methods was a delicate process.

Before starting the research I gained ethical approval from the University of Birmingham and I had to clarify that I was seeking to interview those from predominantly Christian or agnostic/atheist backgrounds and would, despite my own Christian commitment, be non-judgemental about the interviewees' personal religious views. I also had to amend the consent letter in response to comments from the ethical review committee to explain that I am fluent in Welsh and to gain explicit permission to translate the conversations. I also had to state that I had taken great care in order not to put pressure inadvertently on friends or colleagues, to ensure that all approached me rather than me approaching them, to further safeguard the issue of freely given consent. I also had to give assurances of my own professionalism and in respect for boundaries between myself as researcher and my other roles.

The research conversations

In addition to my explanation in the introduction, I would also add that I decided not to follow a formal Biographic Narrative Interview (BNIM)[42] approach (Wengraf, 2000: 141), however I deliberately did not interrupt after my first question and allowed for long silences if necessary, in order to allow the participant to structure the story in their own way. I also prompted with non-verbal cues in order to encourage them to speak for as long as they wanted. I kept the tone of the interviews informal and as close to a normal conversation as possible in order to aid the storytelling process. I responded to questions and also shared my own experience if this seemed appropriate. Porter (1999) discusses her own self-disclosure within research, acknowledging that she would speak about herself when:

> I felt this would not get in the way of the woman talking about herself; how much it would in fact help the woman to express herself; and the extent to which I felt I 'owed' it to the woman in response to her self-disclosure. (1999: 95)

It is debatable within feminist research how much the researcher should disclose about herself. I took the view that I wanted the research conversations to be as naturalistic as possible; therefore if it was appropriate I shared some of my own experience and would express shock, disgust or laugh with the participants. In other words I responded 'normally' and empathetically. In this I took my cue from the participant. Having been an ordained minister for just over twenty years I have gained skills in listening, observing others' body language as well as words in order to ascertain how the other person is experiencing the conversation.

I was also aware of my own failings as an interviewer in my phrasing, sometimes asking leading questions and sometimes contributing too much to the discussion. I would argue that I have to become involved with the conversation in a committed way in order that common meanings and understandings are built. Data from my own reflections were also helpful in analysing the co-construction of the interview. However, I also attempted to be self-aware in interrogating myself as to whether I was accurately reflecting the interview rather than my own interpretation of it through the transcription as well as subsequent analysis.

Strategies for interpretation and analysis

I analysed initially about half of the interviews thematically as I had been asked to contribute a chapter for a book on feminist theological empirical research (Slee, Porter and Phillips, 2013). Although this led to categorising the material prematurely, this did not affect my subsequent interviews greatly as each one was different and unique given that my approach was highly semi-structured.

I identified the following themes mainly because of my own prior interest and because they arose during the first few interviews:

- attitudes to repression and respectability

- positive, ambivalent and negative attitudes towards the self
- positive, ambivalent and negative attitudes towards the Church and religion
- attitudes towards the role of women
- belonging and alienation

I coded each comment which fitted in to the above categories using a free computer programme, Weft QDA, which, after I had coded them for each participant, collected the quotes according to theme. This was useful in identifying commonalities and patterns in the women's stories and reflections.

I chose to analyse the full set of interviews in two stages. The first stage was to look at each life story and interview as a whole and in context, before 'breaking up' the material into themes. This is consonant with an approach which sees the data gained from narratives as holistic, as well as a theological perspective which values the worth of the individual and their unique story. In order to understand each narrative I used insights from discourse analysis, which enabled me to reflect more deeply on issues of identity, nationhood, language and power.

Finally, my five themes for the initial coding became enlarged as I reflected further on the interviews. I found that certain common topics came up unexpectedly for several of the participants: the importance of pastoral care and local church experience, mothering and being mothered, social space and its symbolic significance and the issues of class within the category of belonging and alienation. In writing up the research, I reflected further on how the different categories related to one another and this led to further interpretation on my part. A form of analysis which informed my reflections was discourse analysis, which I now explore.

Discourse analysis and its use in this project

Discourse analysis (DA) is the study of 'language in use' (Gee, 2011: 6), analysing not just words alone – often referred to as 'texts' (Fairclough, 2003: 3) – but the context in which they occur. DA is a perspective rather than a methodology (van Dijk, 2011) and it is acknowledged that there is a lack of consensus regarding its theoretical basis as well as its practice (Ruiz, 2009: 2). It is possible to distinguish between 'social language' (Gee, 2011: 34) and 'discourse', which can contain social language, but also involves other aspects such as context (Gee, 2011: 6), shared knowledge, body language, objects, clothes, non-linguistic symbols, objects, tools, technologies, times and places (Gee, 2011: 46).

The variations in the theoretical roots of the methodology can be distinguished between methods which study texts in great linguistic detail and those which study broader social themes (Fairclough, 2003: 2). Given that my interest was in shared meanings and how women speak of their identity on a more macro level, I decided early on not to use conversational analysis with its more micro analysis of non-verbal communication (ten Have, 2007: 6), nor the more linguistically focused types of DA.

The analysis of discourse is about 'discerning the rules which "govern" bodies of text and utterances' (Fairclough, 2003: 123) whilst acknowledging that discourses are not just representative of 'reality' but also of commonalities of imagination, hopes and mental maps (Fairclough, 2003: 124). In other words discourses signify the whole of human experience whether physical, emotional, or spiritual and within different time spheres – past, present and future.

An important concept within DA is the 'figured world' which is similar to the concepts of 'episteme', 'habitus' or 'imagined community' to describe an imagined, socially constructed sphere or domain (Gee, 2011: 70), where there are commonly recognised social norms, practices and values. The phrase refers to both ideal and normative behaviour as well as value judgements on how people think, act and speak.

One form of analysing the data, therefore, was to interrogate the research participant's 'figured world', by looking at assumptions, phrases and 'typical stories', as well as the people, practices and entities that seemed important to them (Gee, 2011: 72). Any interaction is a mutual process according to discourse analysis, and the work of building, construing and interpreting meaning is something that happens between participants (Gee, 2011: 103).

Fairclough (2003) proposes a scheme (which he freely admits is not definitive or exhaustive) with which to critique language in use. Although I did not follow his scheme to the letter (and it is more accurate to say that these insights have informed my reflective approach rather than giving me a template I followed slavishly), I now outline some of the concepts which I found useful in formulating my own questions with which to interrogate the data. Some of his discourse tools were too specific or detailed for my more macro approach, for example, looking at intertextuality, difference and semantic or grammatical relations between sentences and clauses (Fairclough, 2003: 192–5).

The advantage of using his work as a basis was his enthusiasm for a critical approach that has a beneficial social outcome. He suggests that any analysis begins with an acknowledgement of the issues that have led to the need for analysis, rather than with a traditional research question (Fairclough, 2003: 209). This starting point was also relevant to my project; although I did have a research question, there was a 'social problem' which was prior to it – why did I and why did the women I met in the context of my pastoral and vocational work lack confidence and a sense of their own agency? He also proposes further stages of the researcher reflecting on their own position and on identifying the barriers in dealing with the social problem, whose purposes they serve and how to overcome them (Fairclough, 2003: 209, 210).

Fairclough identifies various tools for DA – for example looking at assumptions and what is not stated (Fairclough, 2003: 11), hegemonic and dialogic language (Fairclough, 2003: 45–9), keywords and metaphors (Fairclough, 2003: 129) and representation of social actors, including themselves (Fairclough, 2003: 145).

Informed by these insights I then formulated a series of questions with which to interrogate the data based on a discourse analytic approach. I did not use these in a sequential way, rather to inform my own reflections.

1. What figured worlds are present here in terms of the individual's identity as female and Welsh? What are the stereotypes, metaphors, archetypes, idealised behaviours and practices of these figured worlds?

2. If religion plays a part in these figured worlds, what form does it take and what impact does it have?

3. What are the key words, metaphors and phrases of the speaker? What do they signify?

4. What are the power relationships implicit in this discourse?

5. What kind of an identity is being enacted here according to Castells's schema – a legitimising identity (extending and giving a theoretical or common sense explanation for their domination), a resistance identity (stigmatised but resilient) or project identity (one which is in the process of being transformed into a positive and enhanced identity for the stigmatised group)? (Castells, 2010: 8).

6. What are the assumptions behind the story and comments?

This analytic approach and these questions, also informed my reflections on the writings I studied as well as my research conversations.

Summary

I have outlined my own commitment to qualitative research and, in particular, to a feminist and reflexive approach which is consonant with my own personal commitments. These have led me to make particular decisions about the research design, which included narrative methods and the insights of discourse analysis. These approaches, I have argued, are particularly relevant for a research project which explores social and personal identity within a culture which values stories and language.

Notes

1 My methodology is fully explained in the appendix.
2 Other researchers have focused on the older generation (for example in the *Merched y Wawr* oral history project I referred to in Chapter 4 and the work of Baker and Brown 2009). Brown (2001) suggests that it is this generation of women who have changed in their attitudes towards religion, especially church attendance.
3 See also Department of Sociology, University of Maryland *Rosenberg Self Esteem Scale* [online], available from *http://www.socy.umd.edu/quick-links/rosenberg-self-esteem-scale* [accessed 1 December 2014].
4 This poem is unpublished.
5 She later attempts to triangulate her findings with quantitative research (with a colleague) (Trosset and Caulkins, 2001) by testing various scenarios with other participants to see if Trosset has accurately identified them as being characteristically Welsh. It is ironic that despite the narrative and thoughtful approach that is a strength of the book, Trosset turns to a quantitative approach with her colleague to substantiate her findings and to investigate stereotyped accounts of Welshness.
6 Welsh Government, Knowledge and Analytic Services (2012), *2011 Census: First Results for Ethnicity, National Identity and Religion for Wales. Statistical Bulletin*, 17 December 2012.
7 All the statistics are from the Welsh Government, Knowledge and Analytic Services (2012), *2011 Census: First Results for Ethnicity, National Identity and Religion for Wales. Statistical Bulletin*, 17 December 2012.
8 Bradley (2007) addresses Ireland and Wales in a chapter in his book *Believing in Britain* looking at the 'Celtic' nations; the linking of these two nations is curious given their very different religious histories.
9 Day (2011) notes that this phrase was initiated, not by Davie, but by Gallup, G. and Jones, S. (1989), *100 questions and answers*, Princeton, NJ: Princeton Research Center.
10 Day, A. (2012), *A Good Day for Census Christians* [online], available from *http://abbydayblog.wordpress.com/2012/12/11/good-day-for-census-christians/* [accessed 4 December 2014].
11 According to The Presbyterian Church of Wales, *What We Do: Ministry*, available from *http://www.ebcpcw.org.uk/english/what-we-do/ministry* [accessed 23 April 2015].
12 According to Jean Gorey, information officer at the Church in Wales Representative Body, in response to a phone call on 23 April 2015.
13 Bruce comments: 'With remarkable tenacity, chapel stalwarts cling to their buildings until dilapidation forces their hand, despite there being so little of theological substance or ritual practice to separate them that they can share services' (2010: 233).
14 Vosper's 1908 painting of Sian Ty'n y Fawnog and her shawl was bought by Lord Leverhulme in 1909 and became popular when prints were given away for vouchers from Lever Brothers' Sunlight Soap; it is currently held in the Lady Lever Art Gallery, Liverpool, see *http://www.liverpoolmuseums.org.uk/ladylever/collections/paintings/gallery4/salem.aspx* [accessed 5 December 2014].

15 Lady Lever Art Gallery (n.d.), *Salem 1908* [online], available from *http://www.liver-poolmuseums.org.uk/ladylever/collections/paintings/gallery4/salem.aspx* [accessed 2 September 2014].

16 Hanes Merched Cymru (2002), *Prosiect Hanes Llafar Menywod yng Nghymru 1920–1960* (Oral History Project Women in Wales 1920–1960) [online], Trinity College Carmarthen and St Fagan's National History Museum, Cardiff, available from *http://www.hanesmerchedcymru.merchedywawr.com/hamdden.html* [accessed 2 September 2014].

17 Hanes Merched Cymru (2002), *Prosiect Hanes Llafar Menywod yng Nghymru 1920–1960* (Oral History Project Women in Wales 1920–1960) [online], Trinity College Carmarthen and St Fagan's National History Museum, Cardiff, available from *http://www.hanesmerchedcymru.merchedywawr.com/hamdden.html* [accessed 3 September 2014].

18 Christine Kinsey Artist/Arlunydd (n.d.), *Ymddiddan/Colloquy* [online], available from *http://www.christinekinsey.com/gallery/* [accessed 31 May 2017].

19 Hanes Merched Cymru (2002), *Prosiect Hanes Llafar Menywod yng Nghymru 1920–1960* (Oral History Project Women in Wales 1920–1960) [online], Trinity College Carmarthen and St Fagan's National History Museum, Cardiff, available from *http://www.hanesmerchedcymru.merchedywawr.com/hamdden.html* [accessed 19 April 2009].

20 The National Library of Wales (n.d.), *Reports of the Commissioners of Inquiry into the State of Education in Wales 1847* [online], available from *http://www.llgc.org.uk/index.php?id=774* [accessed 17 April 2009], pp. iii, 67, 68.

21 The National Library of Wales (n.d.), Saunders Lewis *Tynged yr Iaith: Darlith Radio Flynyddol BBC Cymru*, darlledwyd 13 Chwefror 1962. *Fate of the Language: Annual Radio Lecture BBC Cymru*, broadcast on 13 February 1962 [online], available from *http://www.llgc.org.uk/ymgyrchu/Iaith/TyngedIaith/tynged.htm* [accessed 17 April 2009].

22 Wikiquote *How Green Was My Valley* (film) [online], available from *https://en.wikiquote.org/wiki/How_Green_Was_My_Valley_(film)* [accessed 13 January 2017].

23 British Council for Literature (n.d.),*Writers: Menna Elfyn* [online], available from *www. literature.britishcouncil.org* [accessed 5 November 2013].

24 Elfyn, M. (n.d.), 'Menna Elfyn' [online] available from http://mennaelfyn.co.uk/Interview.html [accessed 5/11/13].

25 Thomas, M. W. (n.d.), *The Place of Gender in the Poetry of Gillian Clarke and Menna Elfyn* [online], available from *www.sheerpoetry.co.uk/advanced/dissertations* [accessed 5 November 2013].

26 Funeral.

27 Waiting rooms.

28 Hughes, S. (2016), 'Eight things you only know about the Welsh if you're Welsh' [online], *Daily Telegraph*, available at *http://www.telegraph.co.uk/women/life/eight-things-you-only-know-about-the-welsh-if-youre-welsh/daily telegraph* [accessed 30 January 2017].

29 Ironically, traces of her Irish accent are often noticeable within the film.

30 A direct quote from the film. IMDB (n.d.), *How Green Was My Valley Quotes* [online], available from *http://m.imdb.com/title/tt0033729/quotes?qt=qt0272038* [accessed 2 November 2014].

31 Although the women in my sample did not speak about alternative therapies or refer to 'holistic' practices.

[32] During the period of this study it was illegal for a cleric within the Church in Wales to perform a wedding between members of the same sex or even to perform a service in church for gay couples after a Civil Partnership.

[33] Flick (2014) argues that qualitative research has been formalised since the 1970s and notes the existence of journals, book series, scientific societies from the 1990s/2000s in the US and Germany establishing it as a credible form of research (chapters 1 and 2).

[34] Swinton and Mowat (2006) suggest that 'ideographic truth' is important within PT because 'it is integral to the language of Scripture and Tradition' since God has been experienced in unique events and these events have been life-changing either to the individuals involved, for example Moses and the Burning Bush and the conversion of St Paul, or to presumably human salvation, for example the death and resurrection of Jesus Christ (Swinton and Mowat, 2006: 43).

[35] Finlay and Gough argue that 'reflexivity … [is] a defining feature of qualitative research' (Finlay and Gough, 2003: 117).

[36] Given the sensitive nature and confidentiality of the research conversations, my blog relates directly to the published writing I have explored as well as the broader themes of the research. Any reflections on the interviews have been subject to the strict ethical procedures of the University of Birmingham.

[37] This is, of course, an ideal that is not unproblematic. See the discussion by Ribbens and Edwards (1998: 204) on the difficulty of finding a balance between the researcher acknowledging her position and commitments and making herself 'visible' with the research whilst still providing enough space for the voices of the participants.

[38] Slee even included herself as a subject within her study, on the same basis as all the other participants (2004: 53).

[39] The role of the individual within narrative methodology is complex given that this methodology stems from two recent and possibly contradictory traditions, that of a more holistic and person-centred humanist approach within psychology and sociology and a poststructuralist approach to narratives within the humanities, and differ in how they regard language, subjectivity and the relationship between the individual and society (Squire et al., 2008: 3, 4). These debates are beyond the scope of this book although it is important to acknowledge them. These approaches can be seen as both modern and postmodern, with the person-centred approach more concerned with the agentic unified self and the poststructuralist approach arguing for a self that is fragmented, socially constructed and changing. These divisions need to be held in tension and recognised rather than resolved. The fragmentation of narrative methods and approaches seems to suggest that the mystery of understanding humans with our complexities and contradictions is something that can only in the end be partially described and understood (Andrews et al., 2008: 4). Theoretically, a narrative approach therefore is consonant with my view of identity and the recognition of the tension between a view of identity which sees it (in everyday practice and discourse) as unified and stable, at least within a personal narrative, and a view which sees identity as performative, socially constructed and evolving.

[40] Mishler points to the researcher's non-verbal communication, such as silence, as influencing a respondent's answer, so even if the interviewer is not actually saying anything, she is involved in the co-creation of the story (Mishler, 1986: 57).

[41] '… it is often through the personal, through the articulation of particularity and what seems to be difference, that connection and universality are suddenly revealed. Indeed, one of the early insights of feminist theology was that, like a good novel, poem, or play,

theology best illumines the universal in human experience through attention to the details of human life' (Plaskow and Christ, 1989: 5).

42   The emphasis in BNIM is on allowing the participant to speak uninterrupted for as long as they like, about anything they like, and this narrative is then analysed. The intention is to minimise the researcher's involvement in the story, but as I have previously argued I am not sure that it is possible or desirable to do this, as within narrative research there is an acknowledgement of researcher involvement and the co-constructed nature of narratives.

Reference List

Aaron, J. (1994), 'Finding a Voice in Two Tongues: Gender and Colonization', in Aaron, J., Rees, T., Betts, S. and Vincentelli, M. (1994), *Our Sisters' Land: The Changing Identities of Women in Wales*, Cardiff: University of Wales Press, pp.183–98.

Aaron, J. (1988), *Pur fel y Dur: Y Gymraes yn Llen Menywod y Bedwaredd Ganrif ar Bymtheg*, Cardiff: University of Wales Press.

Aaron, J. (1997), 'Women in Search of a Welsh Identity', *Scottish Affairs*, 18 (Winter).

Aaron, J. and Rees, T. (1994), 'Introduction', in Aaron, J., Rees, T., Betts, S. and Vincentelli, M. (1994), *Our Sisters' Land: The Changing Identities of Women in Wales*, Cardiff: University of Wales Press.

Aaron, J. and Williams, C. (eds) (2005), *Postcolonial Wales*, Cardiff: University of Wales Press.

Althaus-Reid, M. (2000), *Indecent Theology*, London: Routledge.

Allchin, A. M. (1991), *Praise Above All: Discovering the Welsh Tradition*, Cardiff: University of Wales Press.

Alvesson, M. and Skoldberg, K. (2009), *Reflexive Methodology: New Vistas for Qualitative Research*, 2nd edn, London: SAGE. Kindle edition.

Anderson, B. (2006), *Imagined Communities: Reflections on the Origin and Spread of Nationalism*, revised edition, London: Verso. Kindle edition.

Andrews, M., Squire, C. and Tamboukou, M. (eds) (2008), *Doing Narrative Research*, Thousand Oaks, CA: SAGE.

Archer, M. S. (2000), *Being Human: The Problem of Agency*, Cambridge: Cambridge University Press. Kindle edition.

Arnett, J. J. (2014), *Emerging Adulthood: The Winding Road from the Late Teens Through the Twenties*, 2nd ed., Oxford: Oxford University Press. Kindle edition.

Atkinson, R. (1998), *The Life Story Interview*, London: SAGE.

Badone, E. (1995), 'Reviewed work(s): Welshness Performed: Welsh Concepts of Person and Society by Carol Trosset', *American Anthropologist*, New Series, 97/3, 601–2.

Baker, S. and Brown, B. (2009), 'Harbingers of Feminism? Gender, Cultural Capital and Education in Mid-Twentieth-Century Rural Wales', *Gender and Education*, 21/1, 63–79 [accessed 16 January 2009].

Beck, U. (2010), *A God of One's Own*, Cambridge: Polity Press.

Beddoe, D. (1986), 'Images of Welsh Women', in Curtis, T. (ed.), *Wales the Imagined Nation: Essays in Cultural and National Identity*, Bridgend: Poetry Wales Press, pp. 227–38.

Beddoe, D. (2000), *Out of the Shadows: A History of Women in Twentieth-Century Wales*, Cardiff: University of Wales Press.

Bennett Moore, Z. (2002), *Introducing Feminist Perspectives on Pastoral Theology*, London: Sheffield Academic Press.

Bevans, S. B. (2002), *Models of Contextual Theology: Revised and Expanded Edition*, Maryknoll, NY: Orbis Books.

Bold, C. (2012), *Using Narrative in Research*, London: SAGE.

Bons-Storm, R. (1996), *The Incredible Woman: Listening to Women's Silences in Pastoral Care and Counselling*, Nashville, TN: Abingdon Press.

Bradley, I. (2007), *Believing in Britain*, London: I.B.Tauris.

British Council for Literature (n.d.), *Writers: Menna Elfyn*, available from *www. literature. britishcouncil.org* [accessed 5 November 2013].

Brockmeier, J. (2002), 'Remembering and Forgetting: Narrative as Cultural Memory', *Culture & Psychology*, 8/1, 15.

Brookfield, S. (2006), *The Skilful Teacher*, San Francisco: Jossey Bass.

Brooks, S. (2015), *Pam na fu Cymru: Methiant Cenedlaetholdeb Cymraeg*, Cardiff: University of Wales Press.

Brown, B., Baker, S. and Day, G. (2011), 'Lives Beyond Suspicion: Gender and the Construction of Respectability in Mid-Twentieth-Century Rural North Wales', *Sociologia Ruralis*, 51/4, 370–87.

Brown, C. (2001), *The Death of Christian Britain*, London: Routledge.

Bruce, S. (2002), *God is Dead: Secularization in the West*, Oxford: Blackwell.

Bruce, S. (2010), 'Religion in Rural Wales: Four Restudies', *Contemporary Wales*, 23/1. 219–39.

Bussie, J. A. (2007), *The Laughter of the Oppressed: Ethical and Theological Resistance in Wiesel, Morrison and Endo*, New York: T&T Clark.

Burgess, N. (2000), 'A Home-Going Parson ...', *Theology*, 103/811, 37–45.

Butler, J. (1999), *Gender Trouble: Tenth Anniversary Edition*, New York: Routledge.

Castells, M. (2010), *The Power of Identity*, 2nd edn, Malden, MA: Wiley Blackwell.

Ceridwen, M. (2009), 'Silences', in Johnson, C., *Obsessed with Pipework*, 48 (Autumn), p. 16.

Ceridwen, M. (2011a), 'Another Salem', in Fortune-Wood, J., *Envoi*, 158, p. 50.

Ceridwen, M. (2011b), 'Theology Seminar', in Fortune-Wood, J., *Envoi*, 158, p. 50.

Chambers, P. (2011), 'The Changing Face of Religion in Wales', *The Expository Times*, 122/6, 271–9.

Chambers, P. (2008), 'Out of Taste, Out of Time: The Future of Nonconformist Religion in Wales in the Twenty-First Century', *Contemporary Wales*, 21, 86–100.

Chambers, P. (2005), *Religion, Secularization and Social Change in Wales: Congregational Studies in a Post-Christian Society*, Cardiff: University of Wales Press.

Chambers, P. (2003), 'Religious Diversity in Wales', in Williams, C., Evans, N. and O'Leary, P., *A Tolerant Nation? Exploring Ethnic Diversity in Wales*, Cardiff: University of Wales Press, pp.125–38.

Chambers, P. and Thompson, A. (2005a), 'Coming to Terms with the Past: Religion and Identity in Wales', *Social Compass*, 52/3, 337–52.

Chambers, P. and Thompson, A. (2005b), 'Public Religion and Political Change in Wales', *Sociology*, 39/1, 29–46 [accessed 17 April 2009].

Church in Wales (2012), *Church in Wales Review* [online] available from *http://www. churchinwales.org.uk/review/report/* [accessed 5 December 2014].

Creswell, J. W. (2009), *Research Design: Qualitative, Quantitative and Mixed Methods Approaches*, 3rd edn, Thousand Oaks, CA: SAGE. Kindle edition.

Creswell, J. W. (2013), *Qualitative Inquiry and Research Design: Choosing Among Five Approaches*, 3rd edn, Thousand Oaks, CA: SAGE. Kindle edition.

Daly, M. (1986), *Beyond God the Father. Towards a Philosophy of Women's Liberation*, The Women's Press: London.

Davie, G. (1994), *Religion in Britain since 1945: Believing without Belonging*, Oxford: Blackwell.

Davie, G. (2015), *Religion in Britain: A Persistent Paradox*, 2nd edn, Oxford: Wiley Blackwell.

Davies, C. A. (1999), *Reflexive Ethnography: A Guide to Researching Selves and Others*, London: Routledge.

Davies, R. R. (1974), 'Colonial Wales', *Past and Present*, 65/1, 3–23.

Day, A. (2011), *Believing in Belonging: Belief and Social Identity in the Modern World*, Oxford: Oxford University Press.

Day, A. (2012), *Good Day for Census Christians* [online], available from *http://abbyday-blog.wordpress.com/2012/12/11/good-day-for-census-christians/* [accessed 4 December 2014].

Day, G. (2002), *Making Sense of Wales: A Sociological Perspective*, Cardiff: University of Wales Press.

de Beauvoir, S. (1997), *The Second Sex*, London: Vintage.

de Beauvoir, S. (2000), 'One is Not Born a Woman', in Oliver, K. (ed.), *French Feminism Reader*, Lanham, MD: Rowman & Littlefield. Locations 92–662. Kindle edition.

de Cillia, R., Reisigl, M. and Wodak, R. (1999), 'The Discursive Construction of National Identities', *Discourse and Society*, 10/2, 149–73 [accessed 15 August 2009].

Denzin, N. K. and Lincoln, Y. S. (2011), *The SAGE Handbook of Qualitative Research*, 4th edn, Thousand Oaks, CA: SAGE.

Dickinson, H. and Erben, M. (2006), 'Nostalgia and Autobiography: The Past in the Present', *Auto/Biography*, 14, 223–44.

van Dijk, T. A. (ed.) (2011), *Discourse Studies*, 2nd edn, London: SAGE.

Donahaye, J. (2015), *Losing Israel*, Bridgend: Poetry Wales Press.

Dunlap, S. J. (1997), *Counselling Depressed Women*, Louisville, KY: Westminster John Knox Press.

Elfyn, M. (1978), *Stafelloedd Aros*, Llandysul: Gomer.

Elfyn, M. (1991), *O'r Iawn Ryw: Blodeugerdd o Farddoniaeth*, Dinas Powys: Honno.

Elfyn, M. (1994), 'Writing is a Bird in the Hand', in Aaron, J., Rees, T., Betts, S. and Vincentelli, M. (1994), *Our Sisters' Land: The Changing Identities of Women in Wales*, Cardiff: University of Wales Press, pp. 280–6.

Elfyn, M. (1995), *Eucalyptus – Detholiad o Gerddi Selected Poems 1978–1994*, Llandysul: Gwasg Gomer.

Elfyn, M. (1996), *Cell Angel*, Newcastle upon Tyne: Bloodaxe.

Elfyn, M. (2007), *Perfect Blemish / Perffaith Nam, New and Selected Poems 1995–2007*, Newcastle upon Tyne: Bloodaxe.

Elfyn, M. (2010), 'Barddoniaeth Menna Elfyn: Pererindod Bardd', PhD thesis, University of Wales Trinity Saint David. PhD by publication.

Elfyn, M. (2012), *Murmur*, Newcastle upon Tyne: Bloodaxe.

Elfyn, M. (n.d.), *Menna Elfyn*, available from *http://mennaelfyn.co.uk/Interview.html* [accessed 5 November 2013].

Elliott, J. (2005), *Using Narrative in Social Research*, London: SAGE.

England, K. R. L. (1994), *Getting Personal: Reflexivity, Positionality and Feminist Research*, *Professional Geographer*, 46/1, 80–9.

Evans, N. (2010), 'Class', in Mackay, H., *Understanding Contemporary Wales*, Cardiff: University of Wales Press, pp.125–57.

Fairclough, N. (2003), *Analysing Discourse: Textual Analysis for Social Research*, Abingdon: Routledge.

Fanon, F. (2008), *Black Skin White Masks*, 3rd edn, London: Pluto Press.

Fenton, A. (2014), '"I just want to do the right thing." Christening as performance of respect-ability', paper presented at the Symposium on the Faith/Spirituality of Women and Girls,

Queen's Foundation for Ecumenical Theological Education, Birmingham, 24–25 October 2014.

Finlay, L. and Gough, B. (eds) (2003), *Reflexivity, a Practical Guide for Researchers in Health and Social Science*, Oxford: Blackwell. Kindle edition.

Fisk, A. (2014), *Sex, Sin, and Our Selves: Encounters in Feminist Theology and Contemporary Women's Literature*, Eugene, OR: Pickwick Publications.

Flick, U. (2014), *An Introduction to Qualitative Research*, 5th edn, London: SAGE. Kindle edition.

Freeman, M. (1993), *Rewriting the Self: History, Memory, Narrative*, New York: Routledge.

ap Gareth, O. Ll. (2009), *Welshing on Postcolonialism: Complicity and Resistance in the Construction of Welsh Identities*, Aberystwyth: University of Wales.

Gee, J. P. (2011), *An Introduction to Discourse Analysis: Theory and Method*, 3rd edn, New York and London: Routledge.

Giddens, A. (1991), *Modernity and Self-Identity: Self and Society in the Late Modern Age*, Cambridge: Polity Press.

Gill-Austern, B. (1996), 'Love Understood as Self-Sacrifice and Self-Denial: What Does It Do To Women?', in Moessner, J. S. (ed.), *Through the Eyes of Women: Insights for Pastoral Care*, Minneapolis: Fortress Press, pp. 304–21.

Gilligan, C. (1982), *In a Different Voice: Psychological Theory and Women's Development*, Cambridge, MA: Harvard University Press.

Giudici, M. (2012), 'Discourses of Identity in Post-Devolution Wales: The Case of Welsh-Italians', *Contemporary Wales*, 25, 227–46.

Goffman, E. (1959), *The Presentation of Self in Everyday Life*, London: Penguin.

Goffman, E. (1990), *Stigma: Notes on the Management of Spoiled Identity*, Harmondsworth: Penguin.

Gonzales, M.A. (2007), *Created in God's Image: An Introduction to Feminist Theological Anthropology*, Maryknoll, NY: Orbis Books. Kindle edition.

Graham, E. (1993), 'The Sexual Politics of Pastoral Care', in Graham, E. and Halsey, M. (eds), *Life-cycles: Women and Pastoral Care*, London: SPCK, pp. 210–24.

Graham, E. (2000), 'Practical Theology as Transforming Practice', in Woodward, J. and Pattison, S. (eds), *The Blackwell Reader in Pastoral and Practical Theology*, Oxford: Blackwell, pp. 104–17.

Gramich, K. (2007), *Twentieth-Century Women's Writing in Wales: Land, Gender, Belonging*, Cardiff: University of Wales Press.

Gramich, K. and Brennan, C. (2003), *Welsh Women's Poetry 1460–2001: An Anthology*, Dinas Powys: Honno Press.

Hall, S., 'Who needs "Identity"?', in du Gay, P., Evans, J. and Redman, P. (2000), *Identity: a Reader*, London: SAGE, pp. 15–30.

Hallam, H. (2010), 'When a Bardd Meets a Poet: Menna Elfyn and the Displacement of Parallel Facing Texts', in Williams, D. G. (ed.), *Slanderous Tongues: Essays on Welsh Poetry in English 1970-2005*, Bridgend: Seren, pp. 89–111.

Hampson, D. (1990), *Theology and Feminism*, Oxford: Blackwell.

Hanes Merched Cymru (2002), *Prosiect Hanes Llafar Menywod yng Nghymru 1920–1960* (Oral History Project Women in Wales 1920–1960) [online] Trinity College Carmarthen and St Fagan's National History Museum, Cardiff, available from *http://www.hanes-merchedcymru.merchedywawr.com/index.html* [accessed 19 April 2009].

Harvey, J. (1995), *Visual Piety: The Visual Culture of Welsh Nonconformity*, Cardiff: University of Wales Press.

Heelas, P. and Woodhead, L. (eds) with Seel, B., Szerszynski, B. and Tusting, K. (2005), *The Spiritual Revolution: Why Religion is Giving Way to Spirituality*, Oxford: Blackwell.

Hopwood, M. (2015), *Nes Draw*, Llandysul: Gomer.

Hull, J. M. (2006), *Mission-Shaped Church: A Theological Response*, London: SCM. Kindle edition.

Hughes, T. O. (2001), 'Continuity and Conversion: The Concept of a National Church in Twentieth-Century Wales and its relation to the Celtic Church', in Pope, R. (ed.), *Religion and National Identity: Wales and Scotland c. 1700–2000*, Cardiff: University of Wales Press, pp. 123–38.

Hurdley, R. (2013), *Home, Materiality, Memory and Belonging: Keeping Culture*, Basingstoke: Palgrave Macmillan.

Jantzen, G. M. (1998), *Becoming Divine: Towards a Feminist Philosophy of Religion*, Manchester: Manchester University Press.

Jones, B. L. (1963), *Yr Hen Bersoniaid Llengar*, Cardiff: Gwasg yr Eglwys yng Nghymru.

Jones, H. M. (2010), 'Cerddi Dirgel ein Mamau: Darganfod Alice Walker', in Williams, D. G., *Canu Caeth y Cymry a'r Affro Americaniaid*, Llandysul: Gomer.

Jones, R. W. (2005), 'In the Shadow of the First-Born: The Colonial Legacy in Welsh Politics', in Aaron, J. and Williams, C., *Post-Colonial Wales*, Cardiff: University of Wales Press, pp. 23–38.

Jones, R. M. (1992), 'Beyond Identity? The Reconstruction of the Welsh', *The Journal of British Studies*, 31/4, 330–57 [accessed 16 April 2009].

Jones, S. L. and Yarhouse, M. A. (2006), 'Anthropology, Sexuality and Sexual Ethics', in Lints, R., Horton, M. S. and Talbot, M. R., *Personal Identity in Theological Perspective*, Grand Rapids, MI: Eerdmans, pp. 118–36.

Kinsey, C. (2009), 'A Space of Silent Belonging: Artist's Diary', *Planet: The Welsh Internationalist*, 193 (February/March), 33–41.

Kristeva, J. (1982), *Powers of Horror: An Essay on Abjection*, New York: Columbia University Press.

Kristeva, J. (1984), *Revolution in Poetic Language*, New York: Columbia University Press.

Kristeva, J. (1991), *Strangers to Ourselves*, New York: Columbia University Press.

Lady Lever Art Gallery (n.d.), *Salem 1908* [online], available from *http://www.liverpoolmuseums.org.uk/ladylever/collections/paintings/gallery4/salem.aspx* [accessed 2 September 2014].

Lefebvre, H. (1991), *The Production of Space*, Oxford: Blackwell.

Lewis, S. (n.d.), *Tynged yr Iaith: Darlith Radio Flynyddol BBC Cymru*, darlledwyd 13 Chwefror 1962. *Fate of the Language: Annual Radio Lecture BBC Cymru*, broadcast on 13 February 1962 [online], available from *http://www.llgc.org.uk/ymgyrchu/Iaith/TyngedIaith/tynged.htm* [accessed 17 April 2009].

Linde, C. (1993), *Life Stories: the Creation of Coherence*, New York: Oxford University Press.

Loseke, D. (2007), 'The Study of Identity as Cultural, Institutional, Organizational and Personal Narratives: Theoretical and Empirical Integrations', *The Sociological Quarterly*, 48, 661–88.

Lovell, T. (2003), 'Resisting with Authority: Historical Specificity, Agency and the Performative Self', *Theory, Culture & Society*, 20/1, 1–17.

Llewellyn, D. (2015), *Reading, Feminism, and Spirituality: Troubling the Waves*, Basingstoke: Palgrave Macmillan.

Llewellyn, R. (2001), *How Green Was My Valley*, Penguin Classic Edition, London: Penguin.

Llywelyn, D. (1999), *Sacred Place, Chosen People*, Cardiff: University of Wales Press.

Lynch, G. (n.d.), *Sampling* [online], available from *www.kent.ac.uk/religionmethods/documents/Sampling.pdf* [accessed 20 November 2011].

Mannay, D. (2016), 'Who Should Do the Dishes Now? Revisiting Gender and Housework in Contemporary Urban South Wales', in Mannay, D. (ed.), *Our Changing Land: Revisiting Gender, Class and Identity in Contemporary Wales*, Cardiff: University of Wales Press, pp. 65–86.

Marks, Rh. (2013), *'Pe Gallwn, Mi Luniwn Lythyr': Golwg Ar Waith Menna Elfyn*, Cardiff: University of Wales Press.

Martin, D. (2014), *Religion and Power: No Logos Without Mythos*, Farnham: Ashgate. Kindle edition.

McAfee, N. (2004), *Julia Kristeva*, London: Routledge. Kindle edition.

Mishler, E. (1986), *Research Interviewing – Context and Narrative*, Cambridge, MA: Harvard University Press.

Mitchell, R. H. (2011), *Church, Gospel and Empire: How the Politics of Sovereignty Impregnated the West*, Eugene, OR: Wipf and Stock.

Morgan, D. (1999), 'Christianity and National Identity in Twentieth-Century Wales', *Religion, State and Society*, 27/3–4, 327–42.

Morgan, E. (1994), 'Identity and Religion', in Aaron, J., Rees, T., Betts, S. and Vincentelli, M., *Our Sisters' Land: The Changing Identities of Women in Wales*, Cardiff: University of Wales Press, pp. 267–72.

Morgan, P. (1983), 'From a Death to a View: The Hunt for the Welsh Past in the Romantic Period', in Hobsbawm, E. and Ranger, T. (eds), *The Invention of Tradition*, Cambridge: Cambridge University Press. Kindle Edition, pp. 43–100.

Morgan, P. (1986), 'Keeping the Legends Alive', in Curtis, T. (ed.), *Wales the Imagined Nation: Essays in Cultural and National Identity*, Bridgend: Poetry Wales Press, pp. 19–41.

Morley, D. (1999), 'Menna Elfyn', in Sage, L., *The Cambridge Guide to Women's Writing in English*, Cambridge: Cambridge University Press, pp. 217–18.

Morris, D. (1995), 'Review of Welshness Performed, Carol Trosset', *Journal of Multilingual and Multicultural Development*, 16/4.

Morris, J. (2010), *Conundrum (European Road Maps)*, London: Faber & Faber. Kindle edition.

Neuger, C. C. (1999), 'Women and Relationality', in Miller-McLemore, B. J. and Gill-Austern, B. L. (eds), *Feminist and Womanist Pastoral Theology*, Nashville, TN: Abingdon Press, pp. 113–32.

Office for National Statistics (2012), *Religion in England and Wales 2011*, pp. 1–12, *www. ons.gov.uk*.

Oriel Queen's Gallery (n.d.), *Ymddiddan/Colloquy* [online], available from *http://www. orielqueenshallgallery.org.uk/christine-kinsey-2007.html* [accessed 1 September 2014].

Orsi, R. (2005), *Between Heaven and Earth: The Religious Worlds People Make and the Scholars Who Study Them*, Princeton, NJ: Princeton University Press.

Pace, E. (2007), 'Religion as Communications: The Changing Shape of Catholicism in Europe', in Ammerman, N. T. (ed.), *Everyday Religion: Observing Modern Religious Lives*, Oxford: Oxford University Press, pp. 37–49.

Parry, M. C. (2009), 'Daughters of Gwerful Mechain', in Fortune-Wood, J., *Envoi*, 154 (October), p. 32.

Pattison, S. (2000a), *Shame: Theory, Therapy, Theology*, Cambridge: Cambridge University Press.

Pattison, S. (2000b), 'Some Straw for the Bricks: A Basic Introduction to Theological Reflection', in Woodward, J. and Pattison, S. (eds), *The Blackwell Reader in Pastoral and Practical Theology*, Oxford: Blackwell, pp. 135–45.

Pattison, S. (2007), *Seeing Things: Deepening Relations with Visual Artefacts*, London: SCM Press.

Pattison, S. (2008), 'Is Pastoral Care Dead in a Mission Led Church?', *Practical Theology*, 1/1, 7–10.

Pattison, S. and Lynch, G. (2005), 'Pastoral and Practical Theology', in Ford, D. F. with Muers, R., *The Modern Theologians: An Introduction to Christian Theology since 1918*, 3rd edn, Oxford: Blackwell, pp. 408–25.

Pattison, S. and Woodward, J. (2000), 'An Introduction to Pastoral and Practical Theology', in Woodward, J. and Pattison, S. (eds), *The Blackwell Reader in Pastoral and Practical Theology*, Oxford: Blackwell, pp. 1–19.

Peach, L. (2007), *Contemporary Irish and Welsh Women's Fiction: Gender, Desire and Power*, Cardiff: University of Wales Press.

Phillips, A. (2011), *The Faith of Girls*, Farnham: Ashgate.

Phillips, M. (1997), *Wales: Nation and Region*, Llandysul: Gomer.

Pilcher, J. (1993), 'Who Should Do the Dishes: Three Generations of Welsh Women Talking About Men and Housework', in Aaron, J., Rees, T., Betts, S. and Vincentelli, M. (1994), *Our Sisters' Land: The Changing Identities of Women in Wales*, Cardiff: University of Wales Press, pp. 31–47.

Pitchford, S. R. (2001), 'Image Making Movements: Welsh Nationalism and Stereotype Transformation', *Sociological Perspectives*, 44/1, 45–65.

Plaskow, J. and Christ, C. (eds) (1989), *Weaving the Visions. New Patterns in Feminist Spirituality*, San Francisco: Harper & Row.

Plummer, K. (2001), *Documents of Life 2*, London: SAGE.

Porter, F. (1999), *Faith and Feminism: Women's Christian Faith Experience in Northern Ireland*, D.Phil thesis, University of Ulster.

Pwyllgor y Llyfr Emynau Cydenwadol (2001), *Caneuon Ffydd*, Llandysul: Gomer.

Reddie, A. (2009), *Is God Colour Blind?* London: SPCK.

Redman, P. (2000), 'Introduction Part 1', in du Gay, P., Evans, J. and Redman, P. (2000), *Identity: A Reader*, London: SAGE, pp. 9–14.

Rees, T. (1988), 'Changing Patterns of Women's Work in Wales', in *Contemporary Wales*, vol. 2, pp. 119–30.

Reinharz, S. (1992), *Feminist Methods in Social Research*, New York: Oxford University Press.

Reports of the Commissioners of Inquiry into the State of Education in Wales 1847 [online], available from *http://www.llgc.org.uk/index.php?id=774* [accessed 17 April 2009].

Ribbens, J. and Edwards, R. (eds) (1998), *Feminist Dilemmas in Qualitative Research: Public Knowledge and Private Lives*, London: SAGE.

Riessman, C. K. (1993), *Narrative Analysis*, Thousand Oaks, CA: SAGE.

Riessman, C. K. (2002), 'Analysis of Personal Narratives', in Gubrium, J. and Holstein, J. (eds), *Handbook of Interview Research*, Thousand Oaks, CA: SAGE.

Riessman, C. K. (2008), *Narrative Methods for the Human Sciences*, Thousand Oaks, CA: SAGE.

Roberts, D. W. (2013), *The Welsh Revival of 1904: What Happened Next, A Lesson from History*, Smashwords. Kindle edition.

Rosenberg, M. (1965), *Society and the Adolescent Self-Image*, Princeton, NJ: Princeton University Press.

Ruether, R. R. (1999), 'Gender and Redemption in Christian Theological History' Feminist Theology, 7, 98–198.

Ruiz, J. R. (2009), 'Sociological Discourse Analysis: Methods and Logic', *Forum Qualitative Sozialforschung / Forum: Qualitative Social Research* [online], 10/2, available from *http://www.qualitative-research.net/index.php/fqs/article/view/1298/2883* [accessed 30 November 2014].

Said, E. W. (2003), *Orientalism*, reprinted edn, London: Penguin.

Saiving Goldstein, V. (1960), 'The Human Situation: A Feminine View', *The Journal of Religion*, 40/2, 100–12 [accessed 13 September 2007].

Salmon, P. and Riessman, C. K. (2008), 'Looking Back on Narrative Research, an Exchange', in Andrews, M., Squire, C. and Tamboukou, M. (eds) (2008), *Doing Narrative Research*, Thousand Oaks, CA: SAGE, pp. 78–85.

Scheff, T. J. (1994), *Bloody Revenge – Emotions, Nationalism and War*, Lincoln US: *iuniverse.com*.

Scheff, T. J. (1997), *Emotions, the Social Bond and Human Reality: Part/ Whole Analysis*, Cambridge: Cambridge University Press.

Shooter, S. (2012), *How Survivors of Abuse Relate to God*, Farnham: Ashgate. Kindle edition.

Skeggs, B. (1997), *Formations of Class and Gender: Becoming Respectable*, London: SAGE. Kindle edition.

Slee, N. (2004), *Women's Faith Development: Patterns and Processes*, Aldershot: Ashgate.

Slee, N., Porter, F. and Phillips, A. (eds) (2013), *The Faith Lives of Women and Girls: Qualitative Research Perspectives*, Farnham: Ashgate.

Snorton, T. E. (1996), 'The Legacy of the African-American Matriarch: New Perspectives for Pastoral Care', In Moessner, J. S. (ed.) (1996), *Through the Eyes of Women: Insights for Pastoral Care*, Minneapolis: Fortress Press, pp. 50–65.

Squire, C. (2008), 'Experience-centred and Culturally-oriented Approaches to Narrative', in Andrews, M., Squire, C. and Tamboukou, M. (eds), *Doing Narrative Research*, Thousand Oaks, CA: SAGE, pp. 41–63.

Swinton, J. and Mowat, H. (2006), *Practical Theology and Qualitative Research*, London: SCM Press.

Taylor, C. (1989), *Sources of the Self: The Making of the Modern Identity*, Cambridge: Cambridge University Press.

Thomas, A. (2005), '"Maîtres Chez Nous?" Awaiting the Quiet Revolution in Wales', in Aaron, J. and Williams, C., *Post-Colonial Wales*, Cardiff: University of Wales Press, pp. 85–99.

Thomas, M. W. (2007), *In the Shadow of the Pulpit : Literature and Nonconformist Wales*, Cardiff: University of Wales Press.

Thomas, M. W. (n.d.), *The Place of Gender in the Poetry of Gillian Clarke and Menna Elfyn* [online], available from *www.sheerpoetry.co.uk/advanced/dissertations* [accessed 5 November 2013].

Trosset, C. (1993), *Welshness Performed: Welsh Concepts of Person and Society*, London: University of Arizona Press.

Trosset, C. and Caulkins, D. D. (2001), 'Triangulation and Confirmation in the Study of Welsh Concepts of Personhood', *Journal of Anthropological Research*, 57/1, 61–81.

Volf, M. (1996), *Exclusion and Embrace: A Theological Exploration of Identity, Otherness and Reconciliation*, Nashville, TN: Abingdon Press.

Volf, M. (2006), *The End of Memory: Remembering Rightly in a Violent World*, Grand Rapids, MI: Eerdmans. Kindle edition.

Volf, M. (2011), *A Public Faith: How Followers of Christ Should Serve the Common Good*, Grand Rapids, MI: Brazos Press. Kindle edition.

Walker, D. (ed.) (1976), *A History of the Church in Wales*, Penarth: Church in Wales Publications.

Walton, H. (2007), *Literature, Theology and Feminism*, Manchester: Manchester University Press.

Walton, H. (2014), *Writing Methods in Theological Reflection*. London: SCM Press.

Warner, R. (2010), *Secularization and Its Discontents*, London: Continuum. Kindle edition.

Welsh Government, Knowledge and Analytic Services (2012), *2011 Census: First Results for Ethnicity, National Identity and Religion for Wales. Statistical Bulletin*, 17 December 2012.

Wengraf, T. (2000), 'Uncovering the General from Within the Particular: From Contingencies to Typologies in the Understanding of Cases', in Chamberlayne, P., Bornat, J. and Wengraf, T., *The Turn to Biographical Methods in Social Science: Comparative Issues and Examples*, London: Routledge, pp. 140–64.

Williams, C. (2003), 'Social Inclusion and Race Equality in Wales', in Williams, C., Evans, N. and O'Leary, P., *A Tolerant Nation? Exploring Ethnic Diversity in Wales*, Cardiff: University of Wales Press, pp. 139–59.

Williams, C., Evans, N. and O'Leary, P. (eds) (2003), *A Tolerant Nation? Exploring Ethnic Diversity in Wales*, Cardiff: University of Wales Press.

Williams, C. (2005), 'Problematizing Wales: An Exploration in Historiography and Postcoloniality', in Aaron, J. and Williams, C., *Post-Colonial Wales*, Cardiff: University of Wales Press, pp. 3–22.

Williams, C. (2002), *Sugar and Slate*, Aberystwyth: Planet.

Williams, D. G. (2015), *Wales Unchained: Literature, Politics and Identity in the American Century*, Cardiff: University of Wales Press. Kindle edition.

Williams, G. A. (1982), *The Welsh in their History*, London: Croom Helm.

Wodak, R., de Cillia, R., Reisigl, M. and Liebhart, K. (2009), *The Discursive Construction of National Identity*, 2nd edn, Edinburgh: Edinburgh University Press.

Wodak, R. and Meyer, M. (2009), *Methods for Critical Discourse Analysis (Introducing Qualitative Methods series)*, 2nd edn, London: SAGE.

Woodward, K. (2002), *Understanding Identity*, London: Arnold.

World Council of Churches (2005), *Christian Perspectives on Theological Anthropology: A Faith and Order Study Document*, Switzerland: WCC.

Index